ROUTLEDGE LIBRARY EDITIONS: POLITICAL PROTEST

Volume 3

THE CLERKENWELL RIOT

THE CLERKENWELL RIOT
The Killing of Constable Culley

GAVIN THURSTON

LONDON AND NEW YORK

First published in 1967 by George Allen & Unwin Ltd

This edition first published in 2022
by Routledge
2 Park Square, Milton Park, Abingdon, Oxon OX14 4RN

and by Routledge
605 Third Avenue, New York, NY 10158

Routledge is an imprint of the Taylor & Francis Group, an informa business

© 1967 George Allen & Unwin Ltd

All rights reserved. No part of this book may be reprinted or reproduced or utilised in any form or by any electronic, mechanical, or other means, now known or hereafter invented, including photocopying and recording, or in any information storage or retrieval system, without permission in writing from the publishers.

Trademark notice: Product or corporate names may be trademarks or registered trademarks, and are used only for identification and explanation without intent to infringe.

British Library Cataloguing in Publication Data
A catalogue record for this book is available from the British Library

ISBN: 978-1-03-203038-8 (Set)
ISBN: 978-1-00-319086-8 (Set) (ebk)
ISBN: 978-1-03-203077-7 (Volume 3) (hbk)
ISBN: 978-1-03-203078-4 (Volume 3) (pbk)
ISBN: 978-1-00-318657-1 (Volume 3) (ebk)

DOI: 10.4324/9781003186571

Publisher's Note
The publisher has gone to great lengths to ensure the quality of this reprint but points out that some imperfections in the original copies may be apparent.

Disclaimer
The publisher has made every effort to trace copyright holders and would welcome correspondence from those they have been unable to trace.

The Clerkenwell Riot
THE KILLING OF CONSTABLE CULLEY

BY
GAVIN THURSTON

ILLUSTRATED

London
GEORGE ALLEN & UNWIN LTD
RUSKIN HOUSE MUSEUM STREET

FIRST PUBLISHED IN 1967

This book is copyright under the Berne Convention. Apart from any fair dealing for the purpose of private study, research, criticism or review, as permitted under the Copyright Act, 1956, no portion may be reproduced by any process without written permission. Enquiries should be addressed to the publisher

© *George Allen & Unwin Ltd, 1967*

PRINTED IN GREAT BRITAIN
in 11 on 12 point Plantin type
BY C. TINLING AND CO. LTD
LIVERPOOL, LONDON AND PRESCOT

*To My Friends in
the Metropolitan Police*

INTRODUCTION

Human beings, particularly in cities, have often reacted to adversity by rioting. Scenes of arson and violence in various parts of the world are frequently on our television screens, and we are sickened by the uniformly brutal methods of mob control. Large-rumped policemen, heavily armed, lay about them with staves; missiles fly through the air and, sometimes, a blood-dappled corpse is glimpsed lying among the debris. And so it has always been.

This is the story of a small riot. It happened in London, off the Gray's Inn Road, 130 years ago. It was midway in time between the Peterloo massacre and the Chartist riots of the forties and was brought about by similar pressures; the struggle of the have-nots against the haves, with the desire for more say in the country's affairs as the immediate issue. At the time the affair and its repercussions were hotly discussed for weeks. To-day, with the exception of one or two senior police officers, nobody to whom I have spoken had heard of the Cold Bath Fields.

Although the riot lasted only about ten minutes it was attended by the usual social stresses and familiar characters played their parts. But there were unusual features, there was no incendiarism and no pillaging and no member of the public was seriously injured. On the other hand one police officer was killed and two were seriously wounded. It was the first time that the Metropolitan Police had confronted a mob and quelled a civil disturbance armed only with batons, without military aid.

It is a strange but genuine tribute that we take our Metropolitan Police for granted. Their demeanour and methods contrast sharply with those of the riot police of other countries. The recent shooting in London of three police officers while on duty evoked nation-wide shock and universal condemnation of the criminals. But it was not so in 1833 when Constable Robert Culley was stabbed to death at Cold Bath Fields. A jury found his killing justifiable, his funeral was desecrated by hostile crowds and storms of protest about police conduct raged in the Press and at public meetings. In their early years the police were hated; and it is to the credit of those responsible for their organization

Introduction

and training, for over a century, that the police attitude of steadfastness and tolerance *is* taken for granted. Colonel, later Sir Charles, Rowan and Richard Mayne—the first Commissioners—insisted on the highest standards of conduct which have never depreciated. Of course, we hear criticism of police behaviour from time to time, usually from those on the fringe of the criminal classes, sometimes from educated persons with a critical mentality. Comparison with the 1833 period will show how the relationship between police and public has improved although the contrary is often alleged.

The meeting at Cold Bath Fields was organized by a few obscure agitators for the purpose of forming a National Convention of the working classes, and was an early stirring towards the trades union movement. This half-baked affair attracted public notice and, as well as simple working folk, a number of known bad characters, some of them armed, turned up at the prospect of violence. Colonel Rowan was prepared for trouble and dealt with the gathering with precision and firmness.

In all discussions of politics, petitions to Parliament and the passing of triumphant resolutions it is essential never to forget that politics are about people and that life is a person's most precious possession. The centre of this account is the knife wound in Robert Culley's heart, and beside this all else fades into triviality. Could this wound be justified in any way?

On a warm day on the Calthorpe Estate one can almost feel the presence of the crowds: many of the houses are the same as they were in 1833 and the general conformation of the Cold Bath Fields can be made out. One can imagine the shouting and the brickbats and the hot angry faces; around the corner lies the horror of a warm corpse in a yard waiting to be carried upstairs to a small room.

Research is a frustrating procedure, clues lead to dead ends and records are silent on matters which one would expect to be fully documented. It would have been satisfying to trace the subsequent careers of many of those who will be mentioned. What happened to Mee, Stallwood and others? The Coroner, Thomas Stirling, is a shadowy figure—he was elderly at the time of the inquest and his name is not in the records of the Coroners' Society of England and Wales, founded in 1846. There is plenty about the more distinguished figures—Lord Melbourne, Peel,

Introduction

O'Connell, Roebuck and Sir Charles Rowan himself, but we would dearly like to learn the fate of the humbler people.

The search for material, however, brings many friends; requests for information are met with invariable courtesy and, indeed, eagerness to help. Most of the sources for this book are official. I appreciate access to files HO/61/8 and 61/9 in the Public Record Office and for the copies of the original notices of the Cold Bath Fields meeting. Individuals who have helped are Mr R. F. C. Butcher, Librarian at the House of Commons, Mr W. J. Stead, of the Police College, Sir Joseph Simpson, Commissioner of Metropolitan Police, Mr F. E. Heron, Registrar at New Scotland Yard, Mr H. Hurford-James of Watney's, Mr B. Spencer of the London Museum and the Clerks of the Central Criminal Court and the Bow Street Magistrates' Court. Messrs Boulton, Sons and Sandeman lent me the engraving of the Cold Bath Prison and Fields (1814). Mr W. P. Green, of the Metropolitan Police, drew the plan from rough information supplied by me. Mr Maurice Hall took the present-day photographs. The contemporary newspapers, in the British Museum Newspaper Library at Colindale, were indispensable and I must most specially mention *The Times* without which the account of the inquest and trial of Fursey would have been impossible.

Wimbledon, May 1965–September 1966   GAVIN THURSTON

CONTENTS

		page	
	INTRODUCTION	page	ix
I.	*Reform!*		17
II.	*Mobs and Counter-Mobs*		24
III.	*Skirmishes*		35
IV.	*Unlawful Assembly*		40
V.	*The Affray*		50
VI.	*Aftermath*		60
VII.	*A Remarkable Inquest*		68
VIII.	*Some Lurid Testimony*		84
IX.	*Cross Purposes*		95
X.	*An Interlude. Mr Stallwood's Nemesis*		106
XI.	*The Fourth Day of the Inquest*		112
XII.	*The End of the Inquest*		125
XIII.	*After the Verdict*		136
XIV.	*Another Political Meeting*		144
XV.	*The Trial of George Fursey*		153
XVI.	*Celebrations*		164
XVII.	*Assessment of the Affray*		172
	SOURCES		181
	INDEX		183

ILLUSTRATIONS

1.	Cold Bath Prison	*facing page* 32
2a.	Sir Charles Rowan	
b.	Calthorpe Street 1966	33
3a.	Stallwood's balcony 1966	
b.	The Calthorpe Arms 1966	64
4a.	Early Metropolitan Police	
b.	Calthorpe jury banner	65

Map facing page   19

I

Reform!

Since 1948 any adult citizen of the United Kingdom who is not a peer, convict or mental patient has had the right to vote for his chosen Parliamentary candidate. Today it is difficult to realize that this wide enfranchisement is fairly recent and that it was won, step by step, during more than a century. Before 1832 Parliamentary seats were ill-distributed; for example, Devon County returned two members, the same number as the small Borough of Totnes within its boundaries. The right to vote differed between the inhabitants of counties and boroughs; in a county only males possessing freehold property worth more than 40s a year, about one person in fifty, were enfranchized. The right to vote in a borough varied from place to place; in many it was restricted to members of the corporation, who were expected to support a nominee of the Crown or of some wealthy individual who regarded the Parliamentary seat as part of his possessions.

This inequitable representation kept the nation in the landowners' grasp and led, at a time when the tradesmen and manufacturers of the towns were playing an increasing part in the country's prosperity, to widespread dissatisfaction and unrest. In the latter part of the eighteenth century the Whigs, a coterie of far-sighted thinkers with aristocratic connexions, interested themselves in proposals for making the House of Commons truly representative, a movement which became known by the comprehensive term, 'reform'. William Pitt, an ardent reformer, introduced into the House the first Reform Bill in 1785. This Bill, which was thrown out, included clauses for compensating the owners of rotten boroughs. The cause of reform was kept alive by the Whigs in opposition, notably by Charles James Fox, who

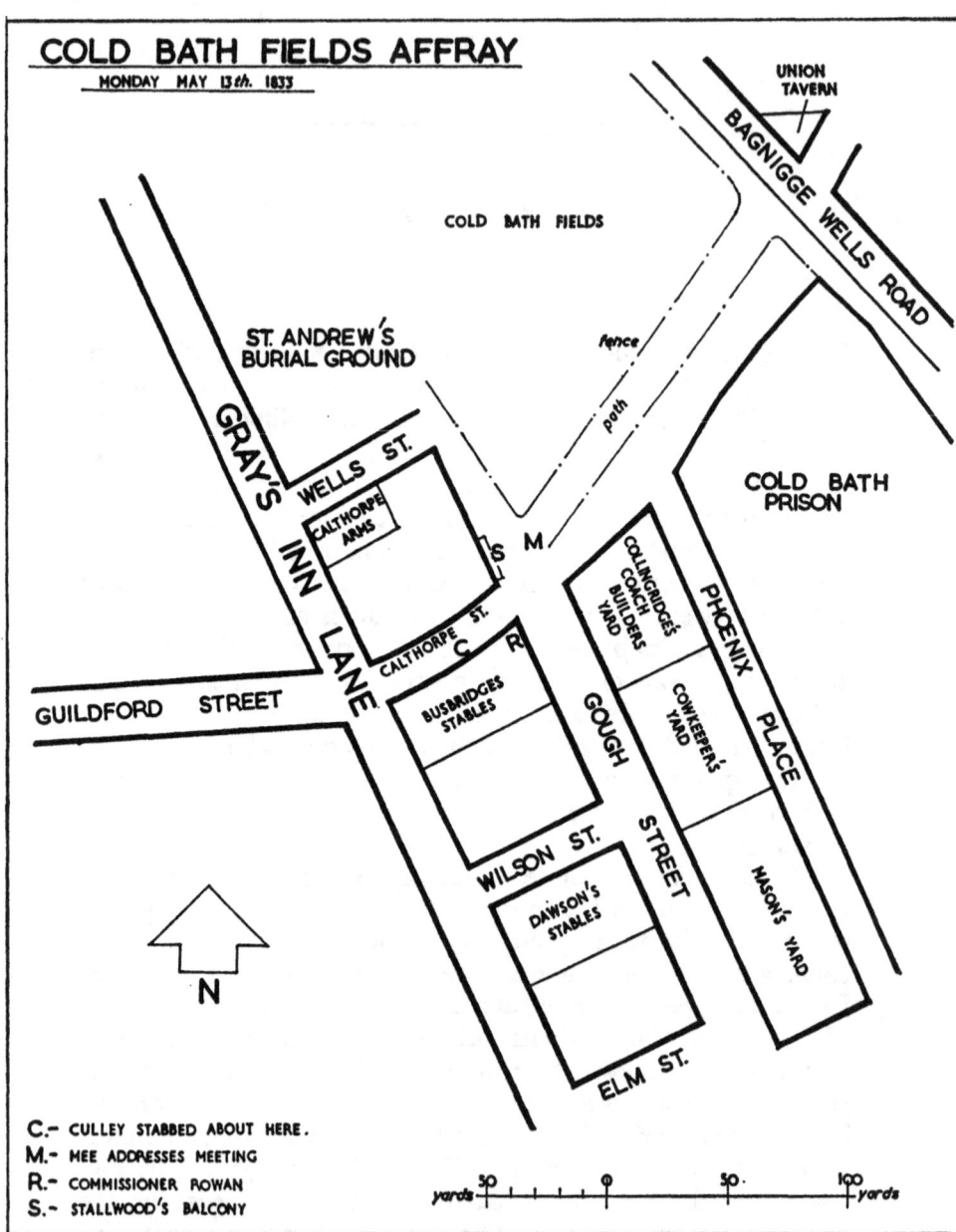

Reform!

died in 1806, and then by Earl Grey, Lord John Russell and others.

When the Whigs came into power in 1830 Lord Grey and his followers had the opportunity to put into practice their theories to reform. The topic was discussed on all sides, opinions differed as to the best way to bring about these changes and the extent to which suffrage should go. There was, however, universal detestation of the rotten boroughs. In 1830 the second Reform Bill passed through the Commons with a huge majority, only to be rejected by the House of Lords. In 1832 a third Bill was introduced and King William IV was persuaded to promise to create sufficient peers to carry the Bill through the Lords. The King then hesitated and commotion occurred in Parliament and throughout the country, focusing attention acutely on the question of reform. These dramatic 'days of May' 1832, culminated in Grey's resignation of his office of Prime Minister. He consented to come back on condition that the King and peers capitulated and at last, sensationally, the long awaited Bill became law as the Representation of the People Act 1832.

The Reform Act 1832 extended the franchise to long leaseholders of property in the counties over the annual value of £10 and to all leaseholders of property over the value of £50. County representation was increased. Borough enfranchisement became uniform and included owners or tenants of any shop, house or other building of annual value above £10. Many boroughs were disfranchised and the seats transferred to the county or to large towns, such as Birmingham. The effect of the Act was to add less than half a million to the electorate in a population of twenty-two millions. There was now one voter in every twenty-five persons instead of one voter in fifty and these new electors were mostly of the affluent middle classes.

For the working classes the long-awaited millennium had not yet come. A hungry, poverty-stricken populace could not be expected to appreciate the constitutional advances made by the Representation of the People Act 1832. Even its title seemed a mockery. The people associated their plight with their lack of influence on the government and were only too ready to take matters into their own hands. The continuing non-enfranchisement of the labouring classes made them into inflammable tinder for the flint and steel of the agitators. Despite Downing

The Clerkenwell Riot

Street's fear of imminent revolution the Whigs and Tories were unwilling to disturb the settlement made by the Act.

Although this account is concerned with the year following the enactment of the Reform Bill of 1832, and particularly with the dispersal of the demonstration in Cold Bath Fields, it is necessary to follow the subsequent progress of reform in order to place the events in their proper perspective. It may well be that the afternoon of May 13, 1833 was the critical time at which the revolutionary fires were damped, never seriously to flare up again in England.

In 1780 Charles James Fox propounded six principles for proper representation of the people in the Commons. They were (1) Manhood suffrage (2) Equal electoral districts (3) Vote by ballot (4) Annual Parliaments (5) Abolition of the property qualification for members of Parliament (6) Payment of members of Parliament. All these propositions have now been fulfilled with the exception of the annual Parliament, which would be impracticable. In 1838 representatives of the working men drew up a People's Charter, which embodied views on reform identical with Fox's. The Charter was received with wild enthusiasm, meetings up and down the country attracted large crowds. Most of the supporters of Chartism favoured peaceable methods of bringing reform; simultaneous withdrawal of deposits from savings banks, refusal to buy excisable articles and cessation of labour were among the measures mooted. Inevitably a section of the community advocated violence and some of the meetings became turbulent. A National Convention of Chartists met in London and in Birmingham in 1839. Although police had successfully broken up the Cold Bath Fields demonstration six years before, the Birmingham authorities again resorted to the military, and collisions with the soldiers infuriated the Chartists and led to fresh rioting. A petition in favour of the Charter was presented to the House of Commons which refused to name a date for its consideration. The National Convention retaliated by recommending general cessation of work. Although this did not take place the state of unrest continued; in November, 1839 at Newport, Monmouth, ten were killed and many injured in disturbances. In 1842 there was further rioting in the north and in the midlands. In 1848 the revolution in France occasioned further Chartist agitation but a much-advertised demonstration at

Reform!

Kennington proved a failure and marked the beginning of the end of Chartism.

After 1848 England entered upon her most prosperous era. Chartism, which was admittedly a 'knife and fork question', waned as employment and wages increased. The trades' unions' gathering influence led to better representation in Parliament of the working mens' difficulties. The original agitators would have been little use as practical politicians; while they could arouse mobs they were too unstable and ignorant to conduct the complicated business of Parliament. Although the Chartists' goals were ultimately achieved by others they played a part in drawing the attention of the legislature to the needs of the working people. The fermenting background undoubtedly hastened the passage of Acts designed to improve social conditions. The Factory and Truck Acts, the Mines Act and the first Public Health Act all reached the statute book during the period of militant Chartism. Finally, the potato famine in Ireland precipitated the repeal of the Corn Laws in 1846 which put cheaper bread into the mouths of the workers and their families.

In 1852 Lord John Russell made an abortive attempt to reopen the subject of reform but there was little pressure from below. The working man wanted food, shelter and work, he was getting these and a modicum of beer and baccy as well and had lost interest in his vote for the time being. In 1867 and 1884 two Representation of the People Acts enfranchised all male householders and lodgers occupying rooms of the annual value of £10 unfurnished. The 1884 Act brought in many farm labourers. The 1867 Act added a million electors and the 1884 Act a further two million. In 1918 women over thirty were given the vote and a uniform qualification for counties and boroughs became law. In 1928 the Representation of the People (Equal Franchise) Act equalized qualifications for men and women and 1948 brought the right to vote to its present position.

The difficulties immediately previous to the Reform Act of 1832 could be ascribed to the growth of the modern industrial state within an agricultural society which till then had had the whip hand. Change is always uncomfortable, to some it is expensive and to others cruel. At the points of resistance bloodshed is certain to occur. King George III was personally opposed to reform which, in the eighteenth century, came to be identified with the revolutionary opinions which led to the American War of Independence of 1775-83 and which were fanning France into flames. America came to be associated with liberty and the rejection of authority.

Today we dread the Fascist and Communist ideologies which seek to rob mankind of the freedom of thought and action which is so precious to the British. The Elizabethans feared the Inquisition of Philip of Spain which set out to impose alien methods of thought. In the early nineteenth century the horrors of the French Revolution and of mob rule were in every Englishman's mind. The explosion of the Revolution in France in 1789 increased public mistrust of reform which was enhanced by the overthrow of the French Legislative Assembly in 1792 and its replacement by the terrible National Convention.

Fearful stories came across the Channel of the misdeeds of Marat, Danton and Robespierre, of the slaughter of Louis XVI and his Queen and of the annihilation of thousands of innocent victims. To understand the mood of government and people in those times it is essential to realize that the shadow of the guillotine was seldom far from their shoulders.

The overthrow of Napoleon in 1815 released thousands of soldiers who roamed the countryside looking for work. Poverty was widespread; high rents for miserable hovels were exacted by landowners, whose pockets were further lined by the hated import duty on foreign corn which raised the price of bread to prohibitive levels. The splendour of the large country estates contrasted too obviously with their agricultural workers' squalid cottages. In London, the mansions of Piccadilly were but a stone's throw from the tenements of Seven Dials. The gulf between rich and poor yawned ominously. Men who had suffered in the wars began to feel that they deserved more than hunger and contumely in the peace. Such attempts as had been made to organize the working classes were pitifully inept and their only Parliamentary representation was through the altruism of reformers such as Cobbett, Grey and Russell. These high minded men had compassion, intelligence and, above all, knowledge of Parliamentary stratagem and manoeuvre but they lacked the driving force of personal experience of the squalor, wrangling and the raw emotions of poverty. It would take several generations to breed men with these requisites.

Reform!

In August 1819 a vast number of working men with women and children gathered together in St Peter's Fields, Manchester, for the purpose of demanding Parliamentary reform. Although the meeting was orderly and peaceful the justices attempted to break it up by sending in mounted members of the militia. These amateurs became the targets of ribaldry from the members of the meeting, the magistrates lost their heads and ordered a charge of cavalry in which eleven were killed and many seriously injured. Although the action of the justices later received governmental endorsement, the nation as a whole was deeply shocked. It may be thought that these humble people did not die in vain and that their involuntary sacrifice gave impetus to the cause of reform; but the field of Peterloo, as it came to be known, has ever since been a symbol of ruthless oppression. The meeting at Peterloo began as a genuine attempt to obtain the vote for the working man, that it ended in disaster was no fault of the organizers. It was followed by years of demonstrations in which agitator-inspired mobs became an embarrassment to government in which the legitimate cause of reform was used to cloak subversive activity of a highly malevolent kind.

II

Mobs and Counter-Mobs

In mankind's communal life laws are essential to the preservation of harmonious relationships. As laws do not keep themselves there must be sanctions to control the misfits and the disaffected. There have always existed men with the talent to incite the misfits and disaffected and fuse them into mobs to defy or overthrow authority. Authority usually prevails, because the will of the majority is behind it. However, authority may be oppressive, corrupt or blatantly profligate; if there is hunger and poverty among the masses the soil is fertile for the agitator's seed. Once an agitator has stirred a mob into riot he can withdraw, leaving loot, drink and fire-raising to finish his task. Order then can only be restored by rigorous official action. If, as was formerly frequent, this takes the form of volley firing or sabre charges and lives are lost the agitator has achieved his object of showing to the world the ruthless brutality of those in power and the people become even more convinced that their rulers must be deposed.

Mob activity was rife in the late eighteenth and early nineteenth centuries. London's growth brought with it vast tenement areas, riddled with passages and cellars in which criminals easily evaded pursuit. The law was represented by parish constables and night watchmen, often old and feeble and at no time a match for a vicious crowd. To prevent import of liquor from abroad the Government encouraged the distilling of spirits in England so that the country was flooded with cheap gin. Hogarth has vividly depicted the terrible effect of drunkenness on the lower classes. The birth rate fell, unemployment was widespread and the corpses of the poor were seen daily in the streets. The cry of loot brought forth howling swarms from the stews and cellars: a sailor who was robbed in a Strand brothel was able to set off an outbreak of pillage and destruction which continued for several days and forced many respectable local inhabitants to evacuate their houses. It was easy for an unscrupulous man to raise a gin-stricken rabble for his own private feuds.

It is said that one of the most skilful exploiters of mob violence of all time was John Wilkes, a cynical self-seeker and a member of Parliament. Although Wilkes has been lauded as a pioneer of modern liberalism, his greater claim to recognition is his unwitting exposure of authority's impotence when faced with rioting. Some historians have gone so far as to suggest that his example inspired the disturbances which led to the American War of Independence and the loss of the American colonies. Wilkes never lacked a host of followers, he even provided blue cockades inscribed 'Wilkes and Liberty'. At times these crowds damaged the carriages and homes of those opposed to his ideas but he always seemed able to control them in the end.

The riots inspired by Lord George Gordon in 1780 were quite a different matter. Gordon was as unbalanced as Wilkes was sane; when he had raised a rabble to protest against a Bill to redress Roman Catholic grievances he found himself unable to halt the outbreak of arson and destruction. All Gordon's protestations and pleas to the King and his ministers could not avail to stop the riots, which raged for a week and wrought untold damage. The military had to be called in to quell the disturbances with volley firing and many lives were lost.

Across the Atlantic, Samuel Adams (not to be confused with John Adams who became President of the Union) quickly realized the power of the mob or, rather, the weakness of the colonial government. Adams, an unsuccessful man who ascribed all his troubles to England, hoped to encompass the downfall of the English Government in the New World. He worked upon the feelings of the numerous poor people in Boston and raised riots in protest against the proposals to levy taxes on the colonists to pay for the recent wars with France. It was at this time, in 1765, that the slogan 'no taxation without represenation', which was to have a familiar ring in the reform movement in England half a century later, was coined. Without appreciating the difficulties of enforcement Parliament passed between 1765 and 1767 a Sugar Act, a Stamp Act and introduced the payment of duty on manufactured articles imported into the American colonies from

The Clerkenwell Riot

England. Adams had no difficulty in still further provoking the enraged colonists. The few parish constables and town marshals were powerless to check the civil disturbances which ensued and the colonial government dared not disperse its troops to deal with sporadic outbreaks of violence. When the Government modified its fiscal demands there was a temporary lull in the disturbances.

In 1770 Adams learned that more troops were coming from England so he immediately assembled large crowds for a mass meeting in Boston. The Governor declared the meetings illegal and issued writs, which led to hoots, laughter and catcalls from the crowds. No military action followed this and other taunts. As there was considerable poverty side by side with wealth in the American colonies, Adams turned his attention to the poor, and organized demonstrations against the rich. He made great play with the concept of 'Liberty' which, he said, meant that no man should be subservient to any superior power on earth, whether direct or legislative. In 1773 the English Government gave the East India Company a monopoly of the tea trade with the colonies in America. This meant abundant cheap tea and the discomfiture of those who made large fortunes from smuggling. The first tea ships to enter Boston harbour were boarded by whooping gangs who threw the tea into the water—the famous Boston Tea Party.

Again Adams had defied authority, which took no steps to seize active control of the situation. England gave the Governor increased powers, took away the Charter given to Massachusetts and insisted on all judicial officers being appointed by the Governor. The trial of any magistrate, soldier or revenue officer for murder in Massachusetts was ordered to be held in London. Still more troops were quartered in Boston. While unemployment and hunger increased, Adams held meetings as and when he pleased. Squads of colonists drilled in the country districts, and arms depots and powder magazines were raided. The public paid no attention to the frequent parades of military parties. The Governor's proclamations against unlawful assemblies were ignored. Anyone who showed the least sympathy with the Government was liable to find his family assaulted and his home set on fire. Finally, the Home Government ordered the arrest of Adams.

In April 1775 it was reported that Adams was expected to stay the night at a house in Lexington, outside Boston. A detach-

Mobs and Counter-Mobs

ment of 800 soldiers was despatched to arrest him, but the noticeable preparations led Revere, one of Adam's supporters, to ride post haste to warn his leader. When the soldiers arrived in Lexington Adams had disappeared but a small party of militiamen was assembled. The English officers ordered them to disperse, they refused, someone fired a musket from behind a hedge and the English opened fire, killing eight men. After nearly ten years of coat-trailing Adams had succeeded in forcing authority to inflict the first serious casualties. On their return journey of eighteen miles the soldiers were sniped at from behind every tree and bush and a relief force from Boston had to be sent to rescue them. Adams is reported to have exclaimed ecstatically 'Oh, what a glorious day is this!'

Hostilities continued in earnest until the capitulation of the English at Yorktown six years later. The Declaration of Independence was signed in 1776.

It is likely that most of the colonists would have been content with a greater degree of self-government under the Crown and the achievement of Dominion status but the ineptitude of authority, together with Adams' mobs, led both sides into the extremes from which they could not draw back and which cost hundreds of lives. Adams himself was a narrow, bitter, bigoted man and, while he played a prominent part in the municipal politics of Massachusetts, his violent prejudice against the statesmanlike Washington prevented his further advancement.

Eight years later the French Revolution broke out.

Based on unemployment, want and hunger the pattern of outbreaks of mob violence showed remarkable constancy. Agitators spread insidious propaganda that the government was to blame for the workers' troubles and drew attention to the spectacle of the rich living in idle luxury. The extravagance of the aristocracy in France was so scandalous that revolution became inevitable. In England and the New World the only agents for law enforcement were the parish constables appointed by the vestries, night watchmen and the American town marshals. It is credibly related that during the Gordon riots a night watchman was seen walking among the screaming mobs and burning buildings calling 'Two o'clock and all's well!' No single person could hope to deal with a riot. When the toll of destruction mounted the only method of restoring order was by the use of troops. While this was effective in the individual disturbance the inescapable loss of life further infuriated the people and provided more ammunition for the agitator. Authority then attempted conciliatory measures, relaxed the severity of laws and possibly remitted taxation and all was well—until the next time.

Unless rioting was brought under control quickly a state of anarchy became established. In France revolutionary leaders were well-prepared and stepped in to form an alternative government. The American colonists were more militarily disposed: many were sturdy woodsmen, well versed in the use of firearms and drilled into disciplined units of militia. The riots soon changed into the organized armed resistance of rebellion. The War of Independence was truly a civil war. Would the same thing happen in England? During the years following Peterloo riots occurred up and down the country but as economic suffering was by no means widespread the outbreaks were confined to one or two areas at a time. The Government was thus able to move troops about without undue dispersal of power. The revolutionaries needed some additional factor to provide common ground for a general uprising of the people. The cry 'Liberty!' had succeeded in France and in America and it appeared that the reform movement might supply a similar motive in England. The agitators accordingly diverted the attention of the working classes to this cause.

As well as the very real threat of revolution the 1820s brought an increase in the commission of crime. It was plain that the system of law enforcement by parish constable was hopelessly inadequate. Over the previous hundred years the introduction of a regular police force had been considered from time to time. Pitt had favoured this in the eighteenth century and the magistrate Henry Fielding had been a strong advocate of the principle of crime prevention rather than detection and punishment: his Bow Street Runners had been a partial success but they were limited to the Bow Street Magistrates' Court. Colquhoun, another magistrate, in about 1800 published *A Treatise on the Police of the Metropolis* which urged that crime could be lessened by a well-organized police force. He founded a small group of Thames police which concerned itself mainly with thefts from the Docks. It was a curious anomaly that concurrently with the spread of crime there should have been strong expressions of hostility to the establishment of police in England. Much of this feeling was due to the example of the French State police under the direction of Fouché. This was the prototype of the totalitarian forces formed for the purpose of forcing the will of the government on the people and was as deeply feared as the Gestapo a century later. In Parliament the law reformers were convinced that all that was needed for crime prevention was the enactment of more humane laws, oblivious of the uncomfortable fact that laws do not keep themselves. The influential City merchants opposed a police force because they found by experience that a system of compounding with thieves, often with the Bow Street Runners as intermediaries, was a practical method of recovering stolen property. They feared the effect of a professional and incorruptible police force on this convenient arrangement. Other sectional interests could see some of their powers being curtailed, among them the revolutionaries whose mob-raising activities might be hampered.

In 1822 Sir Robert Peel became Home Secretary in Lord Liverpool's Tory government. Within a month he took steps to set up a Police Committee to examine the possibilities of establishing a police force. He was astonished by the Committee's adverse report. Either he was unaware of the strong feeling of hostility to the idea of police or he was merely testing the climate of opinion; in either case the rebuff made him lie low for six years, during which period he learned that the Whigs were his most determined antagonists.

When the Police Bill was introduced into the Commons in 1829 the Whigs, surprisingly, offered no opposition to it. Peel had cunningly excluded the City of London, with its strong Whig bonds, from his Metropolitan Police Bill provided that its passage through Parliament was unimpeded. In the years which followed, this political bargain seriously handicapped the effective policing of London. On June 19, 1829 the Metropolitan Police Act became law. While Peel has received most of the credit for the creation of the modern police officer, whose familiar names 'Bobby' and 'Peeler' came from his own, it must be recalled that Fielding, Colquhoun and others had been urging the establishment of an integrated police force for more than half a century. Peel, a legislator of consummate skill, lacked originality and was at his best in moulding other mens' ideas into practical shape.

The Clerkenwell Riot

Even while he was driving the Police Bill through the House he was casting about for suitable men to organize the new force. Wellington was then Prime Minister and it was fitting that the elder of the two chosen Police Commissioners was an officer who had served under him at Waterloo: Lieutenant-Colonel Charles Rowan. The other was an Irish barrister, son of a Judge, Mr Richard Mayne.

It is not unusual to find that with novel legislative conceptions, a preoccupation with the general principles leads to scamping of administrative details. In the Act the powers of the Commissioners were undefined, an omission which caused Rowan and Mayne much difficulty in their early years. The original Metropolitan Police establishment allowed for just over a thousand men: eight Superintendents, twenty inspectors, eighty-eight Sergeants and 895 Constables, together with five clerks. Peel was determined that the new force should be competent and professional, he had no intention of allowing it to degenerate into a sanctuary for the incompetent and the genteel. He wrote that positions were better given to men who had not the rank, habits or station of gentlemen. The Commissioners absorbed the Bow Street foot patrol en bloc and by October, 1829 there were over two thousand applicants.

The Commissioners were determined that only men of the highest character should be considered. They firmly rejected many recommendations from eminent personages, including Wellington, the Duchess of Kent, Melbourne and even Sir Robert Peel himself! It became clear that, despite Peel's intentions, many regarded the new police as a heaven-sent opportunity for off-loading ne'er-do-wells, drunkards and remittance men. Another embarrassment was the respectable tradesman who only intended to remain in the force until he could obtain suitable work in his own line. Within the first two years the Metropolitan Police lost a number of men equivalent to its entire establishment but, gradually, by dogged determination, the Commissioners built up a reliable disciplined force around a nucleus of ex-regular soldiers.

The success of the Metropolitan Police, the surmounting of early obstacles and the implantation of the principles which still permeate all police work are almost wholly due to that remarkable first Commissioner, or Magistrate, as he was sometimes called, Lieutenant-Colonel Charles Rowan. Rowan was, simply and perfectly, a policeman whose dignity and Galahad qualities enabled him to withstand the petty jealousies and political intrigues with which his police were assailed. If he had a fault it was an inability to appreciate the motives and behaviour of lesser men, particularly his own police, and he would not tolerate any departure from the rigid standards which he set up. A portrait in New Scotland Yard depicts an erect military figure, the hair is white and the forehead high. The eyes are calm and steadfast and the nose powerful. There is determination and a hint of obstinacy about the mouth and chin. Rowan's character is highly revelant to an appreciation of the happenings at Cold Bath Fields.

Rowan had spent his working life as an army officer in the 52nd (Oxfordshire) Regiment of Foot. When he joined the 52nd it was commanded by Sir John Moore, whose notions of discipline were at sharp variance with those generally held at the time. It was considered that the object of discipline was to impose, by brutality and repeated floggings, a state of fear which would result in unquestioning obedience to all orders: the soldiers of the time were unintelligent and often drunken and dissolute. Sir John Moore would have none of this, he wanted his men to be God fearing and intelligent, and he inculcated principles of cooperation between officers and men which were regarded as outlandish. He believed that crime in a regiment should be prevented, not barbarously repressed, and that the officers should know their business so thoroughly that unhesitating confidence and respect would pervade all ranks. Practical application of these principles in the 52nd resulted in a high standard of discipline, the cat o'nine tails was never used and the crime rate was low. The 52nd behaved magnificently in Sir John's famous retreat on Corunna. Sir John Moore was a man with a magnetic personality, William Napier wrote of him. 'His was the fire that warmed the coldest nature... No man with a spark of enthusiasm could resist the influence of Moore's great aspirings, his fine presence, his ardent, penetrating genius.'

This was the man who influenced Rowan's impressionable teens and with whom he marched to Corunna. Rowan spent the whole of his army career in the 52nd, he fought through the Peninsular War and was wounded at Waterloo. Following Wellington's great victory, he commanded the Regiment until his retirement in 1822. His occupation for the next seven years, until he was appointed Commissioner of Police in July 1829, is not known.

When Rowan assumed his new command he was unknown in social and political circles. His life had been spent in the comparatively sheltered surroundings of barrack and camp where discipline was simple and codes of behaviour uncomplicated. He was ignorant of the quicksands and undertow of intrigue which lie below the surface of government. He was unaware of the power of the Press to distort and vilify. But his confidence in the importance of his task and his simple religious faith armed him against the onslaughts of those who planned to use the new police as a political football.

Richard Mayne, the other Commissioner, was fourteen years younger than Rowan. As a lawyer he had a sensitive nose for the petty and unworthy motive and proved an excellent complement to the unworldly Rowan. The two men became firm friends and worked in harmony for many years.

Drunkenness among the constables was one of the Commissioners' earliest troubles. The soldiers of the day had a reputation for insobriety, Wellington once sapiently observed when asked what induced men to join the army 'Drink! That and nothing else, you may depend on it'. It was hardly to be expected that all the ex-soldiers who were enrolled in the Metropolitan Police would have the same standards of discipline and temperance as the 52nd Regiment of Foot. Even the careful scrutiny of the Commissioners failed to detect at an interview every rogue recommended to them. As long as it had to be admitted that the constables' behaviour was not always above reproach, the Press had powder and shot for the campaign unremittingly waged against the new police. The undesirables were gradually weeded out but it took time, too much time, at a critical period in police history.

Present-day traffic difficulties were foreshadowed by the total disregard of the well-to-do for the convenience of other road users. Carriages and phaetons were driven and halted as and where they pleased. The police had the unenviable duty of disentangling the resulting congestion at the risk of being deliberately run down or, at least, suffering vicious whip slashes in the face. This public service was held up as yet another example of police interference with 'personal liberty'—in this instance the freedom

1. Cold Bath Prison with Cold Bath Fields in the foreground. (1814).

2. Sir Charles Rowan, First Commissioner of Metropolitan Police

(*Commissioner of Metropolitan Police*)

Calthorpe Street, looking east from Gray's Inn Road 1966

of the rich to behave with arrogance. The Commissioners' task was not assisted by complaints from influential personages whose road behaviour was thus curbed.

It is difficult to understand why there were many disputes and brawls between the police and the military, especially as so many police officers were ex-regular soldiers. Before the formation of the Metropolitan Police the military were often called in to quell rioting but it is improbable that encroachment on this function would be resented by the rank and file. At first Rowan dealt with fights between his men and the military by handing over any soldier concerned to his unit for disciplinary action, but when it became apparent that commanding officers were regarding these assaults lightly the Commissioner changed his tactics and instituted prosecutions in the magistrates' courts.

The magistrates' hostility to the police was infinitely more serious. Although the Commissioners were constituted justices *ex officio* it was never intended that they should exercise a judicial function, the commission being granted to enable them to read the Riot Act if occasion arose. When it became clear that control of rioting was to pass from the magistrates to the police, numerous examples of injustice to police officers in the courts were seen. In the early years of the Metropolitan Police there was no legal branch and the appointment of the Director of Public Prosecutions was many decades ahead. A constable who had arrested a miscreant had to conduct the prosecution himself: for a moderately educated policeman the result of conflict with hostile magistrates, professional lawyers and police-hating juries was a foregone conclusion. Not only would the defendant be discharged against the weight of evidence but the constable might find himself charged with wrongful arrest or assault and convicted with scant ceremony. No funds were available for his defence and his family was likely to starve while he lay in gaol. Even when a finding of guilt was inescapable the lightest possible sentences were imposed. Vicious attacks on police officers went virtually unpunished: the leader of a gang which threw a constable bodily on to spiked railings was fined twenty shillings. Time and again after the most serious injuries had been inflicted on constables the offenders were merely bound over to keep the peace. It says much for the powers of man management of the Commissioners that the force survived at all.

The Clerkenwell Riot

Anyone who has had dealings with local authorities is familiar with civic pride, or parochialism, according to the standpoint of the persons concerned. The parish vestries of the time performed many functions which are now discharged by county or borough authorities. Among these was included the appointment of parish constables. Removal of the police powers was fiercely resented and led to agitation for the abolition of the new police. In addition, it had been enacted that eightpence in the pound out of the parish rates should be paid to the Receiver of Metropolitan Police. This added more fuel to the fire and some parishes attempted to withhold the police rate from the Receiver but the Home Office, for once, supported the police and insisted on prompt payment.

Finally, the revolutionaries saw clearly that the police force was to be a menace to their rabble-rousing activities. They feared the resolute and stalwart police who always seemed to materialize when a seditious meeting or march was arranged. Past masters of whispering campaigns, they lost no opportunity to spread tales of brutalities and oppressions alleged to have been perpetrated by the police. These stories were willingly repeated by the criminal classes, garnished with increasing horrors as they passed from mouth to mouth.

III

Skirmishes

Although a hundred and thirty years ago the Metropolitan Police spent more time on mob control than it does today the multifarious duties of dealing with thieves, drunkards, harlots and the numerous assaults of a turbulent age also went on incessantly. An incident which occasioned correspondence between the Commissioners and the Home Office concerned a herd of cattle found wandering in the streets of Mayfair early one morning. After a resourceful police constable had driven the herd to the station the explanation of this pastoral incursion came to light: the drover, an employee of Lord Lucan, was discovered fornicating with a prostitute in a public square. The magistrates discharged both the drover and his tarnished Amaryllis on the grounds that poverty had driven the woman to desperation.

In November, 1830, the Government learned of a plot to assassinate King William IV on his way to a City banquet; on the advice of his Ministers the King cancelled the visit. This plot was plainly the work of political extremists, the Ultra-Radicals, or 'Ultras' as they were usually known. Peel took the opportunity of referring to the constantly fomented opposition to the Police and produced in the House of Commons samples of a handbill which had been distributed in thousands in the London Streets.

'LIBERTY OR DEATH! BRITONS! ! AND HONEST MEN! ! ! The time has at last arrived. All London meets on Tuesday. We assure you from ocular demonstration that 6,000 cutlasses have been removed from the Tower for the use of Peel's bloody gang. Remember the cursed speech from the throne! ! These damned police are now to be armed. Englishmen, will you put up with this?'

The Clerkenwell Riot

Liberty was the theme of the time: the uneducated could not realize that no member of a civilized community can ever do exactly as he pleases. But it had a fine ring and a man could be encouraged to die for it even if he did not comprehend its meaning. Of course, neither then nor at any time have the English Police been armed with any weapon other than the short wooden baton, which is rarely seen by members of the public. Rowan was acutely conscious of past mortal injuries inflicted by soldiers, when attacking crowds, and he resolved that his men should use the mildest possible methods. Some of his early instructions illustrate his attitude.

'June 3, 1830. The Commissioners have to draw the attention of the whole force to the frequent recurrence of charges of *"obstructing police officers in the performance of their duty"* The Commissioners wish to discourage this practice, and expressly state, that the Police Constable is not authorized to take anyone into custody without being able to prove some specific act by which the law has been broken. No Constable is justified in depriving anyone of his liberty for words only and language, however violent, towards the Police Constable himself, is not to be noticed; the Constables are particularly cautioned not to answer angrily, or enter into altercation with any person while on duty. A Constable who allows himself to be irritated by any language whatsoever shows that he has not a command of his temper, which is absolutely necessary in an officer vested with such extensive powers by law.'

'August 21, 1830. The Constables are to recollect on all occasions, that they are required to execute their duty with good temper and discretion; any instance of unnecessary violence by them, in striking a party in their charge, will be severely punished. A Constable must not use his staff because the party in his custody is violent in behaviour or language. The Constables are not to use a language towards parties in their custody calculated to provoke or offend them; such conduct often creates a resistance in the party, and a hostile feeling amongst the persons present towards the Constable.'

'November 1, 1830. The Commissioners again think it right to caution every man in the Police Force, at a time when an

Skirmishes

attempt is made to create a strong prejudice against them, that they should do their duty with every possible moderation and forbearance, and that they should not furnish a just ground of complaint against themselves by any misconduct.'

Modern methods of mob control are based on the fundamental principles evolved by the Commissioners in those formative and troubled years. For a soldier Rowan showed, at first, remarkable mildness in crowd dispersal tactics. The early drill consisted in lining either side of a street down which a hostile crowd was advancing. There was no attack by Police who simply stood firm and defended themselves if assaulted. Naturally, many were injured by flying brickbats and their tempers were tried to the utmost. Mobs, unable to distinguish between forbearance and cowardice, jeered at the passive constables. However, gradually Rowan increased his aggressiveness, largely as the result of suggestions from a moderate radical, Francis Place.

Francis Place, born in 1771, was a remarkable figure of his time. He started adult life as a leather breeches maker and soon became concerned with the political organization of his trade. This led him to the study of reform, of which he became an ardent supporter. For a time he gave up politics and devoted himself to business as a tailor, in which he was very successful, earning £3,000 in one year—a sizeable fortune for the early part of the nineteenth century. He read avidly every available work on politics and social improvement and amassed a large library at his house at 16 Charing Cross, which became the acknowledged meeting place for reformers, both in and out of office. Sir Samuel Romilly, a lawyer and reformer, wrote

'Place is a very extraordinary person. Self-educated, he has learned a great deal, has a very strong natural understanding and possesses great influence in Westminster—such influence as almost to determine the elections for Members of Parliament.'

Content to be the *eminence grise* Place shunned publicity. Although he was no speaker himself he supplied others with detailed information on every conceivable subject. He produced a number of very dull memoranda and pamphlets and a long history of reform, which was never printed.

The Clerkenwell Riot

Those with moderate views have always found the extremists to be a thorn in the flesh; Place, who believed in reform by peaceful methods, feared the harm which the ebullient Ultras might do to the Radical cause. He saw at once that the Police were his most effective ally against his embarrassing associates, as they would quell the riots without involving Place at all. Accordingly, he cultivated Rowan and Mayne who, in their turn, were glad to have such a valuable source of information.

It was Place, the tailor, who pointed out to Rowan, the soldier, that attack is the best form of defence. Instead of providing a docile target for missiles, why didn't the Commissioner try the effect of baton charges before a mob had a chance to become knit together?

Despite the cancellation of the King's attendance at the Lord Mayor's banquet on November 9, 1830 a huge crowd gathered inside Temple Bar. The bargain which Peel had struck with the Whigs to ease the passage of the Police Bill through Parliament was bearing unwelcome fruit. By excluding the City of London from the Metropolitan Police area, the Act had provided a sanctuary into which the Police could not penetrate in order to prevent the formation of hostile crowds, or assess the size of a mob. On this occasion the people armed themselves with wood and stones from the Public Record Office in Chancery Lane, then in course of construction. Rowan's police were further down the Strand, near Charing Cross. He formed his men into a column and, as the mob advanced down the street, he gave the order to move forward. The rioters were quickly dispersed and fled to the security of the City boundaries. None were seriously hurt and Rowan had demonstrated that police, in solid formation, were more than a match for a much larger undisciplined mob. A week after this triumph the Government fell and the Whigs assumed office. Earl Grey was Prime Minister and Lord Melbourne Home Secretary.

As far as the Police were concerned King Log had been superseded by King Stork. Now in power, the Whigs found themselves in a quandary. In opposition they had persistently opposed the establishment of a Metropolitan Police Force and had only refrained from hindering the Bill in its passage through Parliament because of Peel's unfortunately adroit political bargain. It was common talk that some Whigs had mooted the abolition of the

Skirmishes

Force once they had came into power. But Rowan, who had had a year to organize the Metropolitan Police, had demonstrated its ability bloodlessly to control civil disturbance. No government dared disband this body which had so conclusively proved its worth. Although the Whigs decided to make a show of siding with the public against the police and, in private, to make no bones about their dislike, any proposals to curtail police powers were adroitly side-stepped. Peel had been a lukewarm supporter in trouble, under Melbourne the Commissioners found themselves without any support at all.

Another year of striving between police and mobs passed. Always the rioters played a game of Tom Tiddler's ground, retreating into the City when opposed in strength. As the police were physically incapable of mustering in force at every scene of disturbance crowd damage was unavoidable—on one occasion the windows of Apsley House itself were shattered by stones. On November 7, 1831 an abortive meeting organized by the Ultra-Radicals took place. It may be surmized that Francis Place had a hand in conveying information of this meeting to the Commissioner hoping that the plans of his embarrassing left group would be frustrated without positive action on his part. The meeting was to be held at White Conduit House, Finsbury, arms were to be carried and there was a likelihood of incitement to violence. Colonel Rowan for the first time adopted the principle that prevention is better than cure and posted police at the advertised meeting place. The collection of the crowd was effectively prevented, a further step in the practice of mob control. By routing a mob in Finsbury Square in April 1832 the Metropolitan Police once more gained ascendancy over the forces of disorder.

In the provinces, where there were no police forces, the military were still called in to control crowds. Deaths of bystanders from volley firing and sabre charges were to continue for another ten to fifteen years, well into the Chartist period. Rowan was to participate in his second Waterloo at Cold Bath Fields a year later. No sabres, no firearms, no serious injury to members of the public but three police officers were to be stabbed, one, Robert Culley, fatally.

IV

Unlawful Assembly

The policeman's lot is certainly not a happy one when he is faced with a potentially disordered crowd of people, for the British tradition of freedom of speech is so sacred that the law has never attempted to limit meetings in any way. A police officer must wait until there is overt disturbance. Freedom of speech includes the right to express controversial opinions, often designed to provoke to violence those holding different views. Many societies conceal subversive aims beneath a veneer of professed idealism; and their opponents are ever ready to send to their meetings hecklers and trouble makers. Although a police officer may be well aware of the true nature of an assembly he can do nothing to prevent its occurrence, so long as the highway stays unobstructed. In 1833 the law relating to unlawful assembly was even less settled than it is today. In 1832 Tindal, CJ, reaffirmed the principle of freedom of speech by laying down that a meeting first in the field and lawfully assembled should have preferential treatment over a counterdemonstration.

An assembly is unlawful if three or more persons meet for a purpose which may involve violence, or give rise to the fear of violence in the minds of reasonably firm men. No one, not even a Secretary of State, can declare a meeting unlawful in advance unless it is advertised for promotion of criminal activity. Apprehension of unlawful assembly might arise from the exhibition of banners or badges, from carrying weapons or from the general bearing of those present. The attendance of a speaker who has provoked disorder on previous occasions could arouse the belief that this would be repeated. The senior police officer at the scene, possibly with the assistance of a magistrate, is the judge of the

Unlawful Assembly

nature of the meeting, whether it should be broken up and the amount of force which is to be used.

Riot is an offence both at common law and by statute. The common law definition is similar to that of unlawful assembly, the essential ingredient being behaviour which alarms one person of reasonable firmness. Following the accession of George I rioting broke out on a scale which led to the enactment of the Riot Act 1714. By promoting the offence from misdemeanour to felony in certain circumstances the Act enabled the authorities to use stronger measures in restoring order and to impose heavier penalties. If twelve or more persons are gathered together and do not disperse within an hour of a justice of the peace reading—or attempting to read—a prescribed proclamation, their offence becomes a felony and punishable by life imprisonment; in 1833 it was a capital offence. If necessary, deadly weapons can be used to put down a felony whereas less ruthless action would be appropriate to a misdemeanour.

Many people misunderstood the Riot Act. It was widely believed that no action against a mob could be taken until an hour after the Riot Act had been read. During the Gordon Riots of 1780 troops postponed action against rioters who were looting and burning buildings over the period of the statutory hour. In fact, the Act did not affect the common law powers of dispersal.

The common law offence of affray is committed when two or more persons fight together to the terror of subjects of the Crown.

An interesting statute is the Seditious Meetings Act 1817, passed when the shadow of revolution menaced the country. The Act declared illegal any meeting of more than fifty persons for the purpose of petitioning for alteration of matters in church or state if held within a mile of Westminster Hall during the sitting of Parliament. It is probable that the organizers of the Cold Bath Fields meeting were aware of this statute, for the Fields lie about three miles from Westminster Hall and Parliament was in session on May 13, 1833.

So the decision to disperse falls to the senior police officer on the spot. This has to be done in the full knowledge that he may have to justify his actions later, and that he is steering a dangerous course between the Scylla of his seniors' displeasure at allowing things to get out of hand, and the Charybdis of public and Parliamentary outcry against alleged brutality in suppressing the work-

A PUBLIC MEETING,

Will be held on the CALTHORPE ESTATE,

Cold Bath Fields,

ON MONDAY NEXT, MAY 13, 1833, at TWO o'Clock, to adopt preparatory Measures for holding a

NATIONAL CONVENTION,

The only means of Obtaining and Securing the

RIGHTS OF THE PEOPLE.

By Order of the Committee of the National Union of the Working Classes,

JOHN RUSSELL, Sec.

Lee, Printer, 24, Crawford St.

ing man's right to speak. In the sober conditions of a court of inquiry it is not easy to recreate the atmosphere of a riotous gathering, which includes known bad characters, and stones flying and glass shattering. At such an inquiry there are always trouble makers anxious to exaggerate and misrepresent the police officer's actions. Knowing all this, the officer must still do his duty.

During the week before May 13, 1833 large printed notices appeared on walls all over London. They announced a meeting to be held at Cold Bath Fields.

Colonel Rowan and Mr Mayne, who were kept informed of the activities of the National Union of the Working Classes, at once conferred with inspectors from the outlying police divisions. They learned that meetings of the local groups or classes of the National Union were taking place. The membership of the classes varied between 80 and 130. The meetings, usually held in public houses, were attended by men of desperate character, whose principles were thoroughly subversive of all existing institutions. Language of the most inflammatory sort was used, to give opportunity for them to put into effect such principles. Hatred of the police was excited in all ways, all were advised and encouraged to arm themselves and to resist the police. Both Commissioners were convinced that the meeting at Cold Bath Fields was intended to confront the police in a trial of strength with the Ultra Radicals. If the extremists had even partial success the safety of the whole population of London might be jeopardized. Colonel Rowan decided to visit Cold Bath Fields to make a preliminary reconnaissance.

In 1697 a well was sunk in the Parish of St Pancras, to the west of Clerkenwell Hill. The water was so cold and clear that it became known as the Cold Bath Well, a name which persisted long after the well itself was built over and forgotten. The River Fleet ran to the east of Cold Bath Fields and sometimes overflowed and seeped into the nearby Bagnigge House. In 1760 two springs appeared, one chalybeate and the other purgative. As the springs were about forty yards apart the water was carried through conduits to a small temple, where it was served to customers. For sixty years Londoners walked or drove to the fashionable Bagnigge Wells to drink the water, gossip and take tea in arbours of honeysuckle and climbing roses. The social tone of

The Clerkenwell Riot

Bagnigge Wells gradually deteriorated and by May, 1833 the gardens were in decay but the alternative name of Spafields was still sometimes used for Cold Bath Fields. Cold Bath Prison, built in 1794 and closed in 1877, lay to the south on a site now almost exactly occupied by the Mount Pleasant sorting office. The area was bounded on the west by Gray's Inn Lane, now Gray's Inn Road, and on the east by Bagnigge Wells Road, now King's Cross Road. The essential conformation of the neighbourhood is still discernible and the block between Wells Street, now Wren Street, and the western portion of Calthorpe Street has not changed since 1833—the Calthorpe Arms is the same building! The houses were the first large venture of the celebrated Thomas Cubitt, who built them in 1815, when he was twenty-seven years of age. On the corner of Gough Street and Calthorpe Street is still to be seen a long balcony on the first floor of a house then occupied by a Mr Stallwood, of whom more will be heard: Gough is the family name of Lord Calthorpe. Between Gough Street and Gray's Inn Lane were Busbridge's riding stables and Dawson's livery stables, long since gone. Cold Bath Fields itself was an open patch of waste land, bounded by a simple post and rail fence and sloping downwards at the north-east towards the Union Tavern in Bagnigge Wells Road. A Union Tavern is still on the same site: the distance from Gray's Inn Lane to the Union was about 400 yards.

Rowan habitually rode about London in the sober plain clothes favoured by Wellington's officers, he usually passed unrecognized. After leaving his horse in Busbridge's stables he walked eastwards in Calthorpe Street to the junction with Gough Street. Immediately across Gough Street he noticed the fence around the Fields, the posts were about three feet high and the rails eight to ten feet in length. He decided that this was no serious obstacle and that anyone of moderate agility could vault or duck under it; a heavy press of people would break the fence in an instant.

Rowan satisfied himself that this was a free means of escape for crowds to the north and east across Cold Bath Fields and that the slope down to the Union Tavern would assist such escape. Above all he wished to avoid a hostile mob at bay with no means of retreat. Gough Street was under repair, there were heaps of granite setts which would make admirable ammunition for a mob. Rowan had already caused inquiries to be made about the use of the riding stables as a place of concealment for the police. He confirmed these arrangements with the proprietors of Busbridge's and Dawson's stables. On the corner of Busbridge's stables was a small cottage and from a back window he could command a clear view of Cold Bath Fields and of the proposed meeting ground. He made arrangements to have the use of the room on the afternoon of May 13th.

On the morning of Saturday, May 11, 1833 Lord Melbourne, Home Secretary, Colonel Charles Rowan, Mr Richard Mayne and Mr Samuel March Phillipps, Permanent Undersecretary of State conferred in Lord Melbourne's chambers in Whitehall Gardens, adjacent to Scotland Yard. Lord Melbourne, who later attained fame as the mentor of the youthful Queen Victoria, was a handsome and charming figure. His approach has been described as an exquisite mixture of sarcasm and compliment. He was highly intelligent, indolent and rather a poor speaker. He would have been a difficult character for a man of Rowan's essential simplicity to understand. Melbourne had displayed in his room one of the notices of the Cold Bath Fields meeting. He asked for Rowan's comments. Rowan said there was no doubt that there was a serious threat to law and order. The Metropolitan Police had hampered the raising of mobs by the extremists and sooner or later an organized confrontation was to be anticipated. Rowan had information that many classes of the National Union of the Working Classes had been incited to attend the meeting armed and encouraged to resist the police without scruple.

The following exchange between Lord Melbourne and Colonel Rowan ensued.

'Would not the gallant Commissioner, who has reconnoitred—I believe that is the word?—the battlefield so minutely, deem it advisable to forestall the meeting altogether?'
'I apprehend, my Lord, that there is no legal ground on which we can do this. We are aware of the reports that violence may be contemplated by the unions but, on the face of things, there is insufficient evidence to allow us to place a body of men in advance on Cold Bath Fields.'
'But, my dear Colonel, many of those present are to be armed—cannot the meeting still be anticipated?'

WHEREAS printed Papers have been posted up and distributed in various Parts of the Metropolis, advertizing that a Public Meeting will be held in *Cold Bath Fields*, on *Monday* next, *May* 13th, to adopt preparatory Measures for holding a National Convention, as the only Means of obtaining and securing the Rights of the People:

And whereas a Public Meeting holden for such a Purpose is dangerous to the Public Peace, and illegal:

All Classes of His Majesty's Subjects are hereby warned not to attend such Meeting, nor to take any Part in the Proceedings thereof.

And Notice is hereby given, That the Civil Authorities have strict Orders to maintain and secure the Public Peace, and to apprehend any Persons offending herein, that they may be dealt with according to Law.

By Order of the Secretary of State.

LONDON; Printed by GEORGE EYRE and ANDREW SPOTTISWOODE, Printers to the King's most Excellent Majesty. 1833.

'With respect, my Lord, were we to do this the National Union would merely move elsewhere and collect additional ruffians from the streets as they proceed, leading to the dispersal of our force and making our task the more hazardous.'

'But this is an illegal meeting, cannot you prevent it?'

'Again with respect, my Lord, we cannot declare this meeting illegal on the strength of that poster. We are well aware that it may speedily become so and then we can take action for which, depend upon it, we are well prepared.'

'Well then, when the persons get up and talk about a National Convention, you will know that it is the illegal meeting announced by the placard?'

'That is so, my Lord, but most of the ringleaders are already known to us by sight.'

'Very well, my dear Colonel, you will then arrest the persons attempting to hold the meeting and the crowd will undoubtedly disperse as there will be nothing further to command their attention.'

Colonel Rowan replied, 'I would prefer, my Lord, to be permitted a certain discretion according to the circumstances we find in the field.'

'Naturally, the gallant Commissioner will have my complete trust and I am sure that he will do whatever is expedient to preserve the public order.'

Not a very satisfactory council of war. Rowan was unhappy about the Home Secretary's support. Nothing had been put in writing—with Melbourne it never was. Of one thing he was convinced, this was the testing time when the power of the police over the mob would be tried—they must not fail.

That same afternoon of Saturday, May 11th a messenger from the Home Secretary brought to Scotland Yard a placard for public display. Despite the meeting that morning the Commissioners had been given no hint that such a placard was in the printer's hands. It was headed by the Royal arms.

Mayne's character was more complicated than that of Rowan. As a lawyer he had the capacity to smell out evasions which the straightforward soldier lacked. As a practising barrister he had had experience of interpreting the law in Court, a very different matter from the administrative pronouncements of Whitehall. While both Commissioners were in the situation of the commander in the field who has received, without consultation, an injudicious instruction from the staff, Mayne could see there were certain points in the Secretary of State's notice which could be turned to their advantage.

About two months previously a notice in connexion with a similar meeting had been criticized by politicians on the grounds that it had not been signed. Although Mayne had no doubt that there were no grounds in law for pronouncing the Cold Bath Fields meeting illegal in advance it was clear that it would speedily take on the aspect of unlawful assembly. The notice did, moreover, to some extent take the place of written orders to the Commissioners as to their conduct of the matter. The one thing that was omitted was any reference to dispersal, although it might be inferred that a meeting dubbed 'illegal' should not be permitted to continue. Annoyed at the discourteous lack of confidence shown by the sudden appearance of the Home Secretary's notice the Commissioners went once more to Whitehall Gardens where they saw Mr March Phillipps.

March Phillipps was a superior person who had the irritating habit of speaking in the conditional tense and addressing a point about a foot above the top of his listener's head. Mayne, the Irishman, who had a biting tongue, said forcibly what he thought about the notice.

'It would appear that his Lordship is satisfied about the illegality of this proposed assembly and that is an end of the matter', said March Phillipps. 'At least ye'll have the sense to have these notices signed', Mayne remarked. 'We would not wish to put Lord Melbourne to that trouble but I am personally prepared to sign the notices if that will place them beyond criticism', said Rowan. 'There would appear to be no necessity to trouble you, my dear Sir. In fact, one regrets to say that many of the placards have already been posted.'

There was a short further discussion in which it was revealed that cavalry were to be held in reserve in case the police failed. Rowan and Mayne disapproved of this arrangement but said nothing further.

The next day, Sunday, May 12, 1833 Phillipps received the following note: —

Unlawful Assembly

'Dear Mr Phillipps,

The man who sold the papers (? notices) at Carlisle's shop can be sworn to. Attempts have been made to pull down the Secretary of State's notices and put up more. We have found convenient spots for cavalry and police near the site of the meeting.
     C. Rowan.

      Commissioner.'

V

The Affray

At the Jolly Gardeners, Princes Road, Lambeth Butts on Sunday, May 12, 1833—

'... and so, friends, the time has come, the hour has struck. You are the workers, the producers of the taxes, not the squanderers. We do not give a fig for the Whigs and the Tories, or the man Guelph, the German King. Down with the hereditary aristocracy and up with the aristocracy of the working classes, already united in our National Union. Tomorrow will be your day of glory. Let every man resist the oppressors to the death. Every one of you must go armed. Rally to the flag—Liberty or Death—you and your families have endured starvation and poverty long enough. Arm, arm against the foe. Tomorrow we meet near the new Bedlam and march over Blackfriars Bridge to triumph!'

The forty men present, mostly mechanics, responded with enthusiasm to the agitator, who had been introduced by the chairman of the Lambeth class of the National Union of the Working Classes. The rhetoric was fine, even if they did not understand it, the sentiments were noble and glorious enough to die for. Besides, next day they would subdue the police and overthrow the government. What need of reform, of votes, the working classes would govern for themselves and, led by men like the speaker who thoroughly understood them and knew how to speak, there would be an end to penury.

Weapons were handed round and eagerly examined. There were spring daggers and knives and sticks loaded with lead. There were also some of the peculiar revolutionary weapons devised by Colonel Maceroni for use by crowds against cavalry. The 'Maceroni pike' was about six feet long and hinged in the middle

The Affray

for easy carriage. When the pike was extended a metal sleeve slid over the hinge to increase stability. The blade of the pike was about nine inches long and could be detached and hidden in the clothing and used, if necessary, as a dagger. The butt end was metal shod so that it could be used as a bludgeon when the shaft was folded in two.

The flag with a death's head and the inscription 'Liberty or Death' was proudly exhibited. The speaker gave a final exhortation 'Remember, lads, tomorrow is your day' and left, never to be seen again. Some members of the meeting called for more pots of beer, some went home to give their wives glowing accounts of the prosperous future which lay in store (what their wives thought of the use of weapons is another matter) and one member went back to Lambeth Police Station to report to his superior officer, Superintendent Grimsell. The Superintendent despatched a terse report of the affair to Scotland Yard.

Reports were sent of similar meetings at Bethnal Green, Camberwell, Hammersmith and Islington. At a meeting of class leaders of the National Union of the Working Classes held at Plummer's Hotel, Commercial Road it was agreed that in defiance of the warning of the Secretary of State they were resolved to support the Committee of the National Union in the steps they were taking to secure a convention of the people. In reporting this meeting the Superintendent of K Division underlined the words *'If the meeting takes place the members of the Union will go armed'*.

By the morning of Monday, May 13, 1833 the Commissioners had ample grounds to fear violence at the Cold Bath Fields meeting so one ingredient of unlawful assembly was assured. By about noon a few people were seen on the Fields inside the railings but these could well have been idlers enjoying the warm spring sunshine. One little group reclined on their elbows playing a simple game of tossing pebbles and catching them on the backs of their hands. Two or three plain clothes police officers kept an eye on arrivals, one of these was the police spy Popay, whose activities later brought him the distinction of a select Committee of Inquiry into police spying in general.

The timing of the events which followed is approximate. At an age of unsophisticated pleasure an open air meeting attracted many who looked forward to a sort of show in the company of others, working-class folk who cared little for politics or punctuality. As, from twelve to one o'clock, the ground gradually filled the murmur of voices and laughter rose on the air, which was as soft and warm as fresh milk. A man wearing a new white hat excited passers-by by reciting passages from a publication called the *Reformer* and loudly proclaiming that people in such an emergency ought to carry arms openly: the war drums were beginning to pulsate. One or two men appeared on a long balcony at first floor level of a house on the corner of Gough and Calthorpe Streets. The owner of this house, Mr Nathaniel Stallwood, was the landlord of all the property in the block between Gough Street and Gray's Inn Lane. Mr Stallwood later stated that at this time he was living on independent means and was worth between £40,000 and £50,000. His balcony commanded the whole scene and gave a good view westwards along Calthorpe Street.

Between one and two o'clock it was reported that police parties had arrived and were concealed in Busbridge's and Dawson's stables. The crowd thickened and there was a feeling of excitement as the advertised time for the meeting drew near. Noticeable for his great height, but probably unrecognized, was Colonel de Roos, Brigade Major of the Cavalry Brigade. He was in plain clothes and appeared to be reconnoitring the Fields. By half past two o'clock between 500 and 1,000 had assembled. A humorist took advantage of the ready-made audience to deliver a mock sermon standing on the railings, which delighted his hearers. While it became plain that many were tired of waiting and wondered whether there was to be a proper meeting at all the atmosphere was one of banter and good humour: the conditions were similar to the holiday mood of the crowd at St Peter's Fields, Manchester, fourteen years before.

It was understood that parties of the Unions were coming to the meeting but by half past two none had arrived. The leaders were conferrring in the Union Tavern, Bagnigge Wells Road. It seemed there was a dispute about the procedure and the choice of a chairman, which was regarded as a matter of importance. At about a quarter to three a waggon was seen approaching along the rough track across the Fields from the direction of Bagnigge Wells Road. It stopped at the junction with Gough Street and the six leaders appeared at its tail, it was evident that the waggon was to be the rostrum from which the speeches were to be delivered.

The Affray

A slight young man named Lee waved his hat from the waggon and was greeted by cheers. Then it appeared that there was a dispute with the driver, for, after a short argument, the waggon suddenly drove off depositing the occupants ignominiously in the road. After the leaders had dusted their clothes Lee was born shoulder high to the railings where he supported himself with a piece of board.

'Gentlemen, I propose that Mr Mee be the chairman of this meeting.' About a hundred hands were raised in support of the motion and Mr Mee immediately took his place on the railings, holding on to a lamppost.

Just at this moment shouts, cheers and catcalls announced the arrival of the Union members, who marched up Calthorpe Street with flags and banners flying. They grouped themselves around Mee, the various banners symbolizing the principles for which the meeting was being held. There was a black flag with a red border bearing the skull and crossbones and the motto 'Liberty or Death', an American flag, the tricolour, the Phrygian cap of liberty of the French revolution, 'Holy Alliance of the Working Classes', 'Equal Rights and Equal Justice'. It was a brave show and momentarily inspiring. Mee started to address the tightly packed multitude.

'Beware of those hirelings of the government who are paid to induce you to commit a breach of the peace. We are grateful to the Whigs for advertising our meeting for us, but as the government has threatened you so that in your excitement you may act offensively and so be led to the slaughter be peaceful and orderly. I am only a poor industrious mechanic, but unless you are prepared to pay one-tenth of all your earnings towards the support of my wife and family, do not urge me to go on. If I fall a martyr to the cause and am imprisoned will each of you contribute to the support of my wife and family?'

There were cheers and shouts of 'Go on, go on', 'Aye, that we will'.

'Then I will cheerfully speak my mind'.'

More loud and prolonged cheers and a strong display of enthusiasm.

Said Mee 'Take the flags away'.

The Clerkenwell Riot

There was a murmur of dissent.

'Then take the heads off', he referred to the spikes on the ends of the flag poles.'

'And serves the King so,' shouted Lee loudly.

It was reported that a most fearful shout burst from the lips of the crowd, and showed that the people had been roused almost to a pitch of madness by the revolutionary doctrine which had been inculcated in them by their discussions, and they declared their resolve to meet in spite of law or force.

But suddenly a small cloud passed across the face of the sun, Mee ceased his harangue and turned deathly white. Advancing relentlessly along Calthorpe Street was a solid column of police. The people momentarily appeared to waver and be on the point of breaking when a man in a frock coat, more respectable than the rest of those present, pointed dramatically to the banner and cried 'Liberty or death! Men, be firm' The mob muttered and seethed as he went on 'Down with them, liberty or death!' Others shouted to the speaker 'Go on, go on' but Mee jumped down from the railings and fled, an abortive Spartacus, in the direction of Bagnigge Wells Road, jostling his way vigorously through the press of people.

Freed from even Mee's slender restraint the crowd became belligerent and frenzied, there were cries of 'Come, Englishmen, are we to be trampled on by these bloody Peelers?' Stones began to fly and loaded bludgeons appeared in many hands.

At midday Superintendent Thomas was mustering men of F division of the Police at Bow Street. He had two Inspectors, ten Sergeants and 100 Constables. He had been instructed to be in Busbridge's riding stables by one o'clock. When the men were assembled Thomas addressed them.

'Now, men, you are going out in circumstances that may possibly prove serious. I therefore have to entreat that you will pay particular attention to what I am now saying. Circumstances may possibly bring you into collision with the people—I hope that will not be the case, but should it unhappily turn out so, recollect that the orders of the Commissioners are, at all times, and under all circumstances, to execute your duties with fidelity and firmness, but also with humanity. Don't forget, men, that these are

The Affray

your own countrymen you are going among: therefore, I have to implore you to act with moderation and forbearance. Don't suffer yourselves to be illtreated, but, at the same time, don't use your staves unnecessarily, but as a last resource and as a matter of self-defence'.

There was little secrecy about the destination and intentions of the police. The meeting was well advertised by its promoters, and by the Secretary of State. As they passed through Lincoln's Inn Fields *en route* for Gray's Inn Lane crowds gathered to watch them. Although the unpopularity of the police was apparent from the groans and hisses which marked their progress there were no overt hostile acts. A division was already at Busbridge's stables when F arrived.

The Commissioner, Charles Rowan, came with Colonel de Roos at about half past one and immediately went into the small cottage room overlooking the Cold Bath Fields. Superintendent John May, of A division, in plain clothes, moved between the fields and the Commissioner's room reporting on the assembly as it grew. Superintendent May had served twenty-four years in the Grenadier Guards, seven as a Sergeant-Major, he joined the Metropolitan Police when it was founded and had good experience of crowds. He expressed the view that, while at about two o'clock the crowd was tolerably quiet and well-behaved, he had recognized many bad characters and thought that an ugly situation could very easily develop.

Rowan said to May 'Mr May, as soon as I am satisfied that this meeting is the one which has been advertised you will move in with A division. You will keep the men in column and move up Calthorpe Street. C and F can follow you if necessary and D will come into the Fields from Gough Street. You will keep your men in the carriage way only, leaving the pavements clear for people to escape if they will. You will seize any who appear to be ringleaders and take flags, banners and weapons as evidence. If needs be, the crowd will be dispersed but if you can take the leaders without this so much the better. There will be no violence and no use of staves except in self-defence. Above all, keep the men in a group and do not allow them to separate.'

A cardinal error at Peterloo, in Manchester, fourteen years before was to send the militia separately into a crowd. They were subjected to horseplay, were individually provoked to retaliation and a cavalry charge was ordered to rescue them, with appalling results. The Commissioner well understood the importance of a solid phalanx of men in crowd penetration.

While the men of the police were waiting in the stables permission was given for them to purchase beer. Many of the constables contributed a penny each, and porter was brought from a nearby tavern. About five gallons were shared among seventy-eight men—not much more than half a pint each.

At about ten minutes to three o'clock the din from Gray's Inn Lane heralded the approach of the Unions. Two constables posted at the gate of Busbridge's called into the yard that there was a considerable body approaching with banners at its head. As the Unions passed Dawson's stable they jeered and yelled at C division, which was waiting there, and when they reached Busbridge's someone threw a stone which hit an inspector who was just inside the gate. The constables at the gate recognized the man who had thrown the stone and immediately tackled him, he was brought in and detained. The Unions wheeled into Calthorpe Street where the crowds had become thicker. The cheering was deafening, heads showed at every window and people lined the rooftops. About this time Rowan received a report from the military officer in Collingridge's Coach Works that the wagon was crossing Cold Bath Fields. He saw the wagon halt and then move away again and saw, without being able to hear what was said, Mee hoisted on to the railing. The flags and banners wavered and dipped around Mee.

Superintendent May came in and saluted.

'Sir, that is a man named Mee, a well-known agitator, he has just been elected chairman of the meeting to better the conditions of the working classes.'

'Very well, Mr May, you will move A division, if you please.'

Rowan preceded May out into the stableyard and stood on a chair.

'Now, men, you will be as temperate as possible, there will be no violence and you will secure only those who appear to be leaders and those who offer resistance.'

The order given by May was 'Quick march', about which there was some dispute later.

A division left in column by the Gray's Inn Lane gate of Bus-

The Affray

bridge's stables and wheeled right into Calthorpe Street. The noise was more ominous and boos and groans were blending in with the cheering; stones began to fly. The police column advanced steadily and slowly, it halted about two-thirds of the way down the street by which time there was a clear view of the banners and of Mee standing on the rail. As Mee jumped down the police moved forward again. A constable, John Collis, was hit on the knee by a stone which caused him to stumble and then a brickbat struck him on the back of the head and he fell to the ground, vomiting. The police were now meeting with resistance and batons were coming into use. Constable Angus was confronted with a man with a loaded bludgeon who slashed him across the mouth saying 'Take that, you bloody bugger!' Angus grappled with the man and, with the aid of one of his comrades, held him and took him back to the stables. The police mingled with the banner bearers and endeavoured to take those who appeared to be ringleaders. Some of the Unions retreated across the Fields. Sergeant Tierney, of A division, managed to seize the flag 'Liberty or Death!' and handed the bearer to two of his men. A division was then ordered to open out and follow the mob which was crossing the Fields. It was clear that several pockets of resistance were forming, and the police spread across Cold Bath Fields nearly to Bagnigge Wells Road, breaking up groups of more than four and compelling the people to keep moving. Occasionally youths shouted insults and hurled bricks and stones at the police. Most of these were apprehended.

At three o'clock C division was ordered out of Dawson's stables under the command of Superintendent Baker. The end of Calthorpe Street was obstructed by two or three carts which caused the column to split momentarily. When Baker arrived at the corner he ordered his men to advance with their right shoulders forward. Baker himself was struck on the hand by a brickbat. A dense mob was coming down Calthorpe Street from the direction of Cold Bath Fields; the police column was about twelve men wide and occupied the carriageway. Suddenly a man detached himself from the front of the crowd and thrust at the Superintendent with a weapon like a dagger or the top of a Maceroni pike. Instantly Constable Robert Fawcett stepped up and struck the man with his baton, felling him to the ground. The Constable in turn received a blow on the back of the head which sent him

The Clerkenwell Riot

reeling towards the railings of the houses on the north side of the street. C division continued to press forward and, at the junction with Gough Street, were joined by D division which had come from the back entrance of Busbridge's stables. The scene was confused, with missiles flying through the air and weapons being plied vigorously.

Sergeant John Brooks, on the right of the police column, saw a man carrying a partly furled American flag in his left hand, apparently leading a group of determined rioters. The Sergeant at once laid his hand upon the pole. The man's right hand came up with a brass-handled dagger and struck Brooks in the left chest. Brooks was winded, exclaimed 'Oh!' and recoiled a step or two; he then went on towards the Fields. His flesh was badly lacerated but, fortunately, the blade struck a rib, otherwise it would have pierced his heart. Brooks had a clear view of his assailant and was later able to identify him.

Constable Redwood was just behind Sergeant Brooks and when Brooks was struck he jumped forward and seized the flag with both hands exclaiming 'Come on, my lad, I want that flag'. He loosed his hold when he saw a blade six to eight inches long in the man's right hand. He struck at the man with his baton at the same time holding up his left arm to protect himself. The blade passed right through Redwood's left forearm. Redwood struck the man on the head, seized him and took him into custody. He then handed him over to two constables, Holland and Compton, who took him away. The blow dealt the prisoner by Redwood had lacerated his scalp and blood ran down the side of his face and dripped on to his coat; the two constables hustled him back along Calthorpe Street and into Busbridge's where there was already one prisoner and three or four constables. The prisoners were pushed into a horsestall where they subsided on to a truss of straw.

Meanwhile C division continued to tussle with the rioters in Calthorpe Street. The shouting was deafening and little knots of policemen and Unionists struggled and struck at one another. Somewhere about halfway up the street on the right were Constables Tom Flack, Robert Culley, James McReath and Samuel A'Court, all of C division. As the police moved up the street stones flew through the air and Culley remarked to McReath 'Now for it'. The others lost sight of Culley in the melée. He reap-

The Affray

peared clasping his chest saying to his friend Flack 'Oh, Tom, I am stabbed, I am done'. A'Court replied 'I hope it's not serious, Bob; try and keep up with the division if you can'. At this juncture two men attacked Flack and A'Court, their attention was diverted and they saw no more of Culley.

Culley stumbled, half running back along Calthorpe Street and turned right among the people in Gray's Inn Lane. No one paid him heed for the affray was at its height; one man watching from a window thought he was drunk. Culley turned into the yard of the Calthorpe Arms, fainting, he noticed a group of men and women who looked with horror at the blood streaming from his chest between his fingers. He staggered and as his knees gave he seized the barmaid by the wrist, gasped 'Oh, I am very ill' and collapsed to the ground. The barmaid instantly gathered him into her lap exclaiming 'Oh, you poor lamb'. Culley felt her warm soft breast against his cheek and dimly saw her kind face looking down on him: and beyond that the blue sky in which a few white clouds spun. A trickle of blood ran from the corner of his mouth and he expired.

A local surgeon who had taken shelter in the Calthorpe Arms undid the brave silver buttons on Culley's blue cutaway coat and exposed the coarse flannel shirt saturated in blood. On the bare chest was an irregular wound on the left side into which the surgeon thrust his finger as far as it would go. With the movement more blood flowed from Culley's mouth. 'It must have gone through one of the great vessels. If it had pierced his heart he would not have been able to walk even as far as this', said the doctor.

VI

Aftermath

In ten minutes the meeting had been broken up, several people taken into custody and three policemen stabbed, one fatally. By the time F division, under Superintendent Joseph Thomas, moved into Calthorpe Street in support of C division the affray was nearly over. As the Superintendent halted his division a respectable looking man approached and said that one of his constables had been stabbed. Superintendent Thomas at once went round to the Calthorpe Arms where he saw the body of Culley which he instantly recognized. He then went along Wells Street into Gough Street where he came upon a dozen people below Mr Stallwood's balcony. Mr Stallwood was calling out that the police had behaved disgracefully, that they had acted illegally, that the people were not to blame and that the Riot Act had not been read. One or two members of this small group expressed vicious vengeful threats against the police. The Superintendent repeatedly called upon Mr Stallwood to stop inciting the people.

Thomas said 'You are doing a great deal of harm, pray do not go on so'.

Stallwood excitedly replied 'Why have you not read the Riot Act? Why have you not read the Riot Act?'

'I was not present when the mischief occurred, nor was any of my division'.

Mr Stallwood raged on to such an extent that the Superintendent began to wonder whether he was sober or in his right mind. He continued to address the crowd. Thomas, who had just seen the body of a man who had been stabbed to death, burst out 'It is through such fellows as you that so much mischief is produced. Are you aware that a man has lost his life?'

'No', said Stallwood.

'A policeman has just been murdered'.

Aftermath

'Nonsense, no such thing'.

'Sir, if you will come down, I will show you'.

After a pause Stallwood left his balcony and emerged from his front door. After asking his name he said to the Superintendent 'I have heard of you Mr Thomas; I shall meet you on the police committee, for I am a county magistrate'.

The two men then walked to the Calthorpe Arms where Culley's body still lay in the yard with the wound exposed. 'Is not this a sad sight, Sir?'

Mr Stallwood replied 'It is indeed a sad thing'.

In view of Stallwood's assertion that he was a magistrate Superintendent Thomas felt that it would be prudent to make amends for his earlier peremptory approach.

'Now, Sir, if I have said anything improper to you in the height of feeling I beg to apologize for it'.

'Say no more about it, Thomas, I am quite satisfied'.

The two men shook hands and Thomas returned to his men who were waiting in Calthorpe Street. Apart from a baker who was taken into custody and whose basket of bread was spilled on the roadway there was no further incident.

A smaller detachment of police of N division was stationed in Gray's Inn Lane near the Calthorpe Arms. Even at a little distance from the meeting place the pavements were thronged and there was a buzz of excitement. Three men appeared on the wall of St Andrew's burial ground and started shouting. One called on the mob to slay the police and, if they found them too numerous, to set upon them one by one. The other two threw stones at the police over the heads of the crowd while the speaker brandished a knife. A few constables quickly made their way through the crowd and entered the burial ground. Without any ado amidst hoots and catcalls they dragged the three men off the wall and marched them in custody to Busbridge's livery stables.

Meanwhile Inspector May had instructed the men of A Division to spread in extended order across Cold Bath Fields and prevent any reassembly of members of the crowd. The police moved slowly towards Bagnigge Wells Road breaking up small knots of people who offered little resistance although a number of stones were thrown. One man, William Fursey, who threw stones from the road as the police approached, was arrested. A Division remained on the Fields for about an hour and a half but there was no more disturbance. Bricks and pieces of wood littered Calthorpe Street and there were one or two splashes of blood drying in the warm afternoon. Right through evening to nightfall people stood on doorsteps gossiping and speculating. Knowledge that a man, stabbed to death, lay near by in a familiar public house, made the neighbourhood uneasy.

As prisoners were brought in activity increased in Busbridge's Stables. The main reserve of police was in Dawson's Stables but one or two officers remained in the Stables during the affray and a sergeant had set up a portable table on which he placed a small bottle of ink and some foolscap. He was writing diligently when the men in custody were placed in the stall. He glanced up and noticed that they were reclining half propped up on their elbows. After about fifteen minutes an inspector gave orders that the men should be confined in the coachhouse. After the prisoners had been moved P.C. Hales looked into the stall and noticed some paper with printing on it in the straw. His suspicions were aroused and he hunted through the straw where he found a pistol, a powder flask and a dagger. Only two men had occupied the stall, the man who had stabbed Sergeant Brooks and P.C. Redwood, and another. These articles were handed to the inspector. A number of other prisoners were brought into Busbridge's Stables and held there until the police returned to their various stations. They were then taken to Bow Street Magistrates' Court.

The magistrates sat the same evening, continuing the proceedings far into the night. Presiding was Sir Frederic Roe, an implacable enemy of the police, sitting with Messrs Minshell and Halls. The first prisoner was Robert Tilley, a bricklayer aged twenty of Church Street, Lambeth. He had a dirty bloodstained bandage around his head and complained of being faint from loss of blood. Police Constable Goody stated that the prisoner was advancing in front of a mob in Calthorpe Street and that he had made a blow at Goody with a truncheon; the constable had some difficulty in seizing him but eventually took him into custody. Another constable said that when the pistol found in Busbridge's stables was shown to Tilley he unhesitatingly identified it as his. Police Constable Hales had seen the prisoner and two others brought in and placed in the stall, where they lay down on a pile of straw. He found the pistol, which was loaded, and the powder flask and dagger, all of which were produced. Police Constable

Aftermath

Hales confirmed that he was present when Tilley acknowledged his pistol.

Inspector Clements testified that he had accompanied Robert Tilley in a coach from Busbridge's stable to Bow Street. During the journey Tilley volunteered that he had the truncheon in his pocket to defend himself against the police; the pistol was in case he was attacked by the military.

The magistrates then questioned Tilley, who said that he went to the meeting as other men did who wished to redress their grievances. He knew they wished to form a national convention but what this was he didn't understand. He had been in other rows and riots and said that as he had been previously badly handled by police he took the truncheon to defend himself. The pistol was to protect himself against military attack as the people at Peterloo had done. Tilley denied knowledge of the powder flask and dagger found in the straw. He was remanded for four days.

Tilley's allegations of police violence sound a note familiar at the present day. His artless admissions revealed a standard of intelligence which showed him and his kind as ready dupes for agitators.

The next prisoner, George Fursey, was altogether a more formidable figure. His head, like that of Tilley, was bandaged. He was charged with stabbing P.C. Redwood, which in 1833 was a capital offence. Redwood gave evidence that on that afternoon he was on duty in Calthorpe Street; about 4,000 to 5,000 people were assembled. As P.C. Redwood advanced in front of his division for the purpose of dispersing the mob he saw Fursey holding the American colours in his hand. Redwood told him to deliver up the colours, Fursey refused and Redwood seized him by the collar. Redwood saw the prisoner's right hand raised in the air, holding a long shining blade, and at the same instant he received a stab in the left arm from a sharp instrument. Redwood released the colours but never relaxed his hold on Fursey until he had delivered him over to his fellow officers. A three edged dagger produced in Court was the same as that with which he had been wounded.

As the charge was one which affected the prisoner's life, Sir Frederick Roe said he would not call on him for his defence at that stage. However, before being removed, Fursey denied the charge and complained that he had been struck by the police in the first instance.

Lee was next placed in dock. He said his Christian names were Richard Egan. Police Constable Markwood, on oath, stated that he saw the prisoner addressing the crowd, regretting that they had been deprived of their hustings and moving that Mee should be elected chairman. Markwood described the approach of the classes of the Working Men's Union bearing banners and poles with spikes at the ends of them. Mee cried out 'Take the flags away', someone else exclaimed 'Take the heads off', which the witness understood to refer to the spikes at the end of the poles. The prisoner then cried, 'and serve the King so'.

Lee, who took notes of the evidence, admitted that the witnesses were correct with the exception of the words he was said to have uttered. He had never said anything against the King. Then some pamphlets were produced to which Lee's name, as a printer, was appended. One was entitled 'A Whisper to the Whigs, or, What is Treason?' The prisoner then admitted that he was a printer and that he worked a press in his own house. He was married and aged twenty-four.

Sir Frederick Roe observed that the words uttered by the prisoner Lee were treasonable, he granted bail on Lee's own recognizance of £200, with two further sureties of £100. He would require forty-eight hours' notice of the sureties as it would be necessary to investigate their solvency. Lee was then removed in custody. At the same time James Hutchinson, a carpenter and builder, of number one Tudor Place, Tottenham Court Road was charged with attempting to rescue Lee from the police. He denied the charge, saying that he was merely passing through on his way to Pentonville. He was granted bail.

Less serious charges then followed. John Smith was charged with exciting the mob and throwing stones at the police. Richard Bunn and William Calf with riotous assembly and attempting to incite the mob to violence. Police officers testified that Bunn and Calf were very active in the crowd, Bunn several times called out 'Come, Englishmen, are we to be trampled upon by these bloody Peelers?' and Calf shouted 'Is this the way that Englishmen are served?' They were held to bail in £100 each. Richard Morgan, who himself sometimes acted as parish constable, was charged with throwing a brickbat which struck a constable on the back of

3. Stallwood's balcony in 1966

The Calthorpe Arms in 1966

4. Early Metropolitan Police Officers   (*Commissioner of Metropolitan Police*)

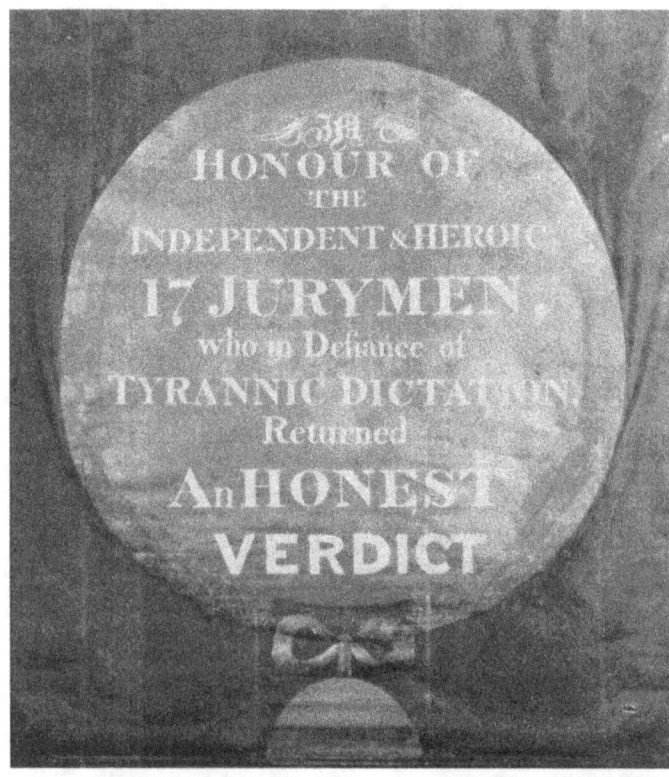

The Calthorpe Jury Banner

(*London Museum*)

Aftermath

the head. There was the usual denial and he was granted bail for £100 and two sureties of £50 each.

William Fursey, brother of George Fursey, had thrown stones at police from the Bagnigge Wells Road, as the mob had by that time dispersed the magistrates fined him forty shillings, or, in default, two months' imprisonment.

Thomas Tilley, brother of the man who admitted to carrying a loaded pistol, was charged with striking Police Constable Andrew Angus with a bludgeon, and knocking him down. The bludgeon was produced, it was about a foot in length and loaded heavily with lead at one end. Thomas Tilley was remanded. The men who appeared on the wall of St Andrew's Burial Ground were next placed in the dock. Police Constable Charles Knott stated that one of them, Roome, called upon the mob to slay the police and if they found them too numerous to single them out one by one and lay them quiet man by man—this was shortly after the policeman was killed. The two other prisoners, Forrest and Hobbs, threw stones and cheered. A case knife was found on Hobbs.

The sexton of St Andrew's, Holborn, George Hicks, came forward and said that Hobbs was one of his grave diggers. He stated vehemently that the police evidence was false and that no such language had been used. The knife, he said, belonged to him, and he supposed that his dog had taken it into the burial ground where it was found by Hobbs, as the dog often carried away bones in the same way. Sir Frederick regarded the story about the dog as incredible and required the three prisoners to find bail in the sum of £100 each. William Davey, a pauper, was convicted of throwing stones at the police and sentenced to two months' imprisonment with hard labour in default of paying the fine of forty shillings. James Edwards, a metal sash maker, was held to bail for the same offence. Three or four others were fined forty shillings for throwing stones.

The proceedings before the magistrates continued until half past eleven at night, afterwards the prisoners were all taken in the prison van to Clerkenwell Prison, closely guarded. The notes of evidence were sent to the Home Secretary's Department.

Hatred and rancour were not all on the side of the working classes. All the prisoners were artisans to whom £100 at 1833 values was an impossible sum. As forty-eight hours' notice was required in all cases to investigate the financial status of sureties all those bailed were condemned to at least two days' imprisonment, even if they were able to find sureties. Sir Frederick Roe knew this as well as he realized that the pauper Davey had no hope of raising his fine. In the circumstances two months' imprisonment with hard labour for throwing stones was a ferocious sentence.

A newspaper report of Wednesday, May 15, 1833 stated that several applications had been made to reduce the amount of bail and to shorten the forty-eight hours' notice to twenty-four hours. Sir Frederick returned a decided negative to these applications, but expressed his readiness to enter into the question of bail in every instance in which the terms of the commitment were complied with. Many of the applicants pressed their claims heatedly and spoke loudly against the injustice of such heavy bail.

On May 15th the *Sun* reported

'This morning the flags and banners which were taken from the people at the meeting yesterday were conveyed by Superintendent Thomas, and an escort of the force, from the chief stationhouse in Bow Street (where they had been deposited during the night) to the Secretary of State's office in Downing Street. The poles upon which the banners were fixed have been constructed in a manner to be immediately turned into a weapon of defence, being joined together in the middle by a hinge whilst strengthened by a sliding tube passing over; thus, by removing the tube, the ends which joined and which could be divided in an instant, could be turned into a weapon of offence or defence, as each end was bound with iron. Some had pike heads, the others were adapted for the same purpose. That on which the cap of liberty was placed had a complete pike head.'

By Thursday, Sergeant Brooks was sufficiently recovered from his wound to give evidence in the resumed hearing of the charge against Fursey. Fursey was described as a tall muscular man about twenty-eight years of age, having a long face and high cheekbones. His appearance was that of a decent mechanic. Although he followed the proceedings anxiously he showed no sign of fear.

Sergeant Brooks described how he was struck in the chest and he identified the dagger produced as that with which he

Aftermath

was stabbed. He identified Fursey as the man who struck the blow. Police Constable Redwood also identified Fursey and stated that he had never loosed his hold of him until he had handed him over to Constables Holland and Compton. Police Constable Hales testified to finding the dagger under the straw. A surgeon described the wounds of Sergeant Brooks and of P.C. Redwood and remarked that only the chance of the blade striking a rib had saved Brooks from being fatally stabbed through the heart. Fursey was committed for trial at the Old Bailey on a charge of unlawfully, feloniously and maliciously stabbing John Brooks and Henry Chance Redwood with intent to do them some bodily injury. He would be hanged if convicted.

The brothers Tilley were brought back into court but being unable to find bail they were returned to the house of correction.

In the Daily Police Report for May 22, 1833 the following information was published.

'Whereas it hath been humbly represented to the King, That, on Monday, the 13th day of May instant, Robert Culley, Police Constable, whilst engaged in the discharge of his duty in dispersing an illegal assemblage of persons in Cold Bath Fields, in the county of Middlesex, was wilfully and maliciously stabbed, by some evil-disposed person unknown, and almost immediately died of the wound so inflicted.

'His Majesty, for the better apprehending and bringing to justice the person who committed the murder before mentioned, is hereby pleased to promise His most gracious Pardon to any one (except the actual perpetrator thereof) who shall discover such person as aforesaid, so that he may be apprehended and convicted of the same murder.

'And, as a further encouragement a Reward of One Hundred Pounds is hereby offered by the Right Honourable the Lords Commissioners of His Majesty's Treasury, to any person (except as aforesaid) who shall make such discovery as before mentioned and convicted thereof.

(signed) Melbourne.'

VII

A Remarkable Inquest

The body of Robert Culley lay in a small room on the first floor of the Calthorpe Arms, awaiting inspection by the coroner and his jury. Originally, as coroner and jury sat around the corpse to hold their inquest, hygienic considerations demanded rapid conclusion of the proceedings: as recently as 1882 a judicial *obiter dictum* recommended opening an inquest within five days of discovery of the body. Although it is no longer necessary for a jury to view the body and refrigeration has done away with one reason for haste, inquests are usually still opened within a few days of report to the coroner.

At the time of the Culley inquest Mr Thomas Stirling, HM Coroner for West Middlesex, was 88 years of age. He was clearly in a hurry to get the affair over and opened the case on Wednesday, May 15th, only two days after Culley's death, and went through to conclusion without any length of adjournment. It would have been prudent to open the case, take evidence of identification, issue a warrant for burial and then adjourn for a week or two. This would have given Mr Stirling time to consider the information available and to reflect on the wider implications of this sensational event. An adjournment would also have given breathing space for emotions to die down a little. It seems unwise to decide to hold the inquest in the Calthorpe Arms, right on top of the scene of the affray. Formerly it was common practice to hold inquests in public houses but, while this was often inescapable in country districts where only inns had suitable accommodation, it seems an unnecessary course in London. The dignity of the inquest proceedings would not be enhanced by association with the atmosphere of the sale of liquor and the type of person who frequented taverns in the early nineteenth century. This impor-

A Remarkable Inquest

tant inquest, which was to attract nationwide attention, was conducted in a manner which can only be described as remarkable.

The lists of occupations of the jurors, drawn from local residents, is of some interest:—

Samuel Stockton,	baker, Cromer Street (Foreman).
John Spalding,	baker, Chichester Place.
Charles Tighe,	upholsterer, Chichester Place.
Benjamin Hastie,	baker, Chichester Place.
Henry Neville,	cornchandler, Chichester Place.
John Bliss,	baker, Chichester Place.
Joseph Burgess,	pawnbroker, Chichester Place.
Thomas Pearson,	ironmonger, Gray's Inn Lane.
John Graham,	grocer, Gray's Inn Lane.
Edward Holder,	glass cutter, Gray's Inn Lane.
Joseph Langran,	cheesemonger, Gray's Inn Lane.
William Purdy,	shoemaker, Gray's Inn Lane.
William Davies,	plumber, Gray's Inn Lane.
John Doller,	broker, Gray's Inn Lane.
George Dennis,	baker, Sidmouth Street.
William Alexander,	auctioneer, Cromer Street.
Robert French,	baker, Calthorpe Street.

Of these seventeen jurors six were bakers. This preponderance may be explained on the custom of bakers starting work very early in the morning and having finished by midday, so that they were available when the coroner's officer went round to pick his jury. With the exception of the brokers and the plumber every member of the jury probably worked in the house in which he lived. As small tradesmen they would not be particularly in sympathy with the National Union but hostility to the police and resentment of the privileged classes was certain. Few were likely to have been enfranchised by the 1832 Reform Act, an additional reason for resentment of authority. A more serious objection to the jurors was that they all lived very near to Cold Bath Fields and it is probable that most of them had seen the affray, discussed it with neighbours and formed some very decided opinions.

A large room on the first floor of the Calthorpe Arms, immediately over the bars, was reserved for the inquest. The windows

The Clerkenwell Riot

looked over both Gray's Inn Lane and Wells Street. On the afternoon of Wednesday, May 15, 1833 the Coroner and jury climbed the dark narrow stairway and viewed the body of Robert Culley in a small room adjacent to the inquest room. Culley had been dead for two days, the weather had been warm and decomposition was beginning. The jury filed into the inquest room, clearly affected by the sight, and took their allotted places. The room was crowded and two magistrates, Jessopp and McWilliam, had come to observe the proceedings. All that afternoon and throughout the subsequent days bystanders thronged the streets and patronized the bars freely. Every time the courtroom door was opened wafts of tobacco smoke came in and the buzz of conversation was a constant background. From time to time bursts of laughter punctuated the hearing.

Mr Nathaniel Stallwood was the first witness. After being sworn he stated that he had been on his balcony from three in the afternoon until late in the evening. He said that his balcony commanded a full view of Cold Bath Fields and the surrounding streets. At about three o'clock a caravan driven by a man named Reynolds, whom he knew, drew up below the balcony and the organizers of the meeting climbed in; it was obvious that this was to be used as a hustings. Then there seemed to be a dispute about payment for Reynolds suddenly drove off with the others still on the caravan. They hurriedly jumped off and Lee then mounted the railing supporting himself with a placard board. He proposed that Mee be the chairman of the meeting. Mee addressed the people before him as gentlemen, because they were the producers and not the consumers of taxes. He was glad that the Government had sent persons to take down what he said, so that there should be no misrepresentation. He was obliged to the Whig Government for advertising the meeting. As Mee's speech continued Stallwood saw a body of police appear at the west end of Calthorpe Street while, at the same time, a second body came from the White Horse Livery Stables, which were Mr Stallwood's property let to Mr Busbridge. This second body of police advanced along Gough Street. All the avenues from the vacant piece of ground were now blocked by police.

'The men in Gough Street were then ordered to draw their staves from their pockets and then directed to charge indiscrim-

A Remarkable Inquest

inately. The two bodies united then began by knocking everybody down, men, women and children. There was no order requesting the people to disperse. The Riot Act was not read, neither was the proclamation read. The ground was covered with bodies lying in all directions. No resistance was made by the crowd at any time, except when a policeman was making his way to the chairman I saw a stout man put his hand against a policeman's breast to stop him, but he was instantly knocked down. The system of knocking everybody down continued for an hour, without any attempt to take any person into custody, which might have been done by any spirited individual with half a dozen policemen, as no person could by any possibility escape, all the avenues being closed. Observing the policemen still continuing to ill-treat the people, I addressed the force from the balcony, desiring them, if the people were doing wrong, to take them into custody; that as the Riot Act had not been read nor the proclamation, nor any opportunity given to the people to disperse, in my opinion the police themselves were the only disturbers of the public peace, and acted illegally. Mr Thomas, the inspector of police, called me a scoundrel, and said it was such men as I encouraged mobs like the present. I immediately demanded his name, which he refused to give. I came down into the street to put two ladies into a carriage from my house. I then demanded Mr Thomas's name, which he gave me, and begged to apologize for the language he had used, as one of their body was already murdered, and which, he said, had very much exasperated him. He then begged that I would attend to see the body, which was at the Calthorpe Arms, and I accompanied him to that house. I there found the body lying on the table, with a slight but sharp wound inflicted on the left side, and which appeared to me to have instantly entered the heart. Mr Thomas again apologized.'

By this time Mr Stallwood was getting well into his rhetorical stride, he addressed the Coroner in a forceful peroration, which should have been stopped as having nothing to do with finding the cause of Culley's death.

'I beg to add, Sir, that the men, women and children who were standing at my door, and on the steps of other doors, were all shamefully beaten. One of my tenants, who attempted to take

The Clerkenwell Riot

refuge in my house, was also beaten. All the people who witnessed the conduct of the police cried shame and expressed their horror at their conduct. The people began to assemble at nine o'clock in the morning, and if the police had not interfered the meeting would not have taken place.'

The inquest had certainly got off to a rousing start and the jurors quickly began to participate.

A juror—'How many persons were assembled?'
Mr Stallwood—'About 300'.
Juror—'And how many policemen came to disperse them?'
Mr Stallwood—'About 300'.
Juror—'The chairman exhorted them to keep the peace?'
Mr Stallwood—'Yes'.
Juror—'Then there would have been no disturbance if the police had not interfered?'
Mr Stallwood—'No'.
Juror—'Do you consider that fifty of the old police could have dispersed them?'
Mr Stallwood—'If I had had the assistance of six men I could have dispersed them, because they were so surrounded I could have gone in and picked out the leaders; they could not escape as the whole of the avenues leading to the ground were blocked up. After I had addressed the police they began to take persons into custody, and the first person whom they took was the boy Lee, who first got up into the waggon.'
Juror—'Every avenue was closed?'
Mr Stallwood—'Yes, every avenue was blocked up, but I am informed that the chairman escaped over the new sewer now making at the back of the house of correction. I could have taken him as easily as possible.'
Juror—'Was it in the power of those who had the command of them to have restricted them?'
Mr Stallwood—'The leaders did not appear to have any command over them, nor did any of the leaders attempt to restrain the men, excepting when Thomas addressed me and called me a scoundrel; then the men gave a "hurrah", but Thomas desired them to desist. The leaders appeared to have no command over the men. The policemen struck without the slightest provocation.

A Remarkable Inquest

They carried their staves in their hands behind them, and in a moment, if a person only turned round, he received a blow, either on the head or legs, which disabled him.'

Several members of the jury murmured 'Shame, Shame.'

Juror—'When Thomas called you a scoundrel the policemen cheered?'

Mr Stallwood—'Yes; but he has made a most ample apology since.'

Juror—'You observed several persons wounded?'

Mr Stallwood—'I saw boys with broken heads, and even with the blood running down them'.

Mr Stallwood then stood down and his place was taken by a Mr Venables, of Lambs Conduit Street, who testified that he saw an elderly man lying on the ground with his head broken. There were also two or three hats without the crowns lying about. When he crossed Cold Bath Fields before the affray he was struck by the peaceable bearing of the people and it astonished him that the attack had been made upon them.

Thomas Baker, Police Superintendent of C Division was next sworn. He said he was on duty at Dawson's livery stables in Gray's Inn Road that Monday afternoon. At about three o'clock he received an order to move his division to Calthorpe Street to assist in dispersing the mob assembled on the waste ground; an assembly which was declared by the Secretary of State to be illegal—the proclamation calling upon the people not to meet and warning them of the consequences that would follow. The Supeintendent had been in charge of their distribution throughout London.

A juror broke in to ask whether there was any name appended to the bill to which Superintendent Baker replied that as far as he was aware there was only one Secretary of State. The Coroner, for once, restrained the juror, saying that it would be better to postpone questioning the witness until he had finished his story.

Superintendent Baker then continued:

'On arriving with my division at the end of Calthorpe Street

The Clerkenwell Riot

about three o'clock, I found an obstruction of two or three carts at the end of the street. My division was then moving in a column of subdivisions, myself at their head, and on arriving at the corner I ordered my men to advance with their right shoulders forward into Calthorpe Street. We had scarcely advanced two yards into the street when I received a blow on my hand from a brickbat. At that time there was a mob coming down the street, and I had not proceeded, I think, to the depth of more than three doors when we came in contact with the head of the mob. One ruffian singled himself out and made a thrust at my breast with a dagger, or something like that. One of my constables, seeing this, sprung forward and struck the ruffian a blow on the head, which prevented him from committing the rash act which he contemplated. The moment he was knocked down the police constable who struck him received a blow on the back of the neck, which sent him towards the railing head foremost. I then pressed forward with my division and saw several stones and brickbats coming at us. At that moment a man was coming forward bearing an American flag, and surrounded and followed by a great number of persons. Several of my constables sprang forward to secure him and the colour, in doing which I heard that two of my constables were stabbed, one named Brooks and the other Redwood, the latter through the left arm, and the former in the left side. They both belonged to the C division. I then proceeded to near the top of Calthorpe Street, close to the open space, and I then halted my division, and ordered the two above-named to go to the rear and get medical assistance. At this instant I heard a cry in the rear that Robert Culley was stabbed. At this moment the open space at the end of Calthorpe Street was cleared, and the mob dispersing in all directions. Leaving my division in Calthorpe Street, I then repaired along the open ground and came round to this house (the Calthorpe Arms), where I found the deceased in the yard, where he had just expired. I sent for Mr Simpson, a medical gentleman, who declared life to be extinct, and I had the body removed upstairs. I then returned to my division in Calthorpe Street, and afterwards went to Mr Busbridge's livery stables, where I found about twenty-four persons in custody. From the time of my arrival in Calthorpe Street first of all, until I saw these men in custody, and the mob was dispersing, not more than twenty minutes had elapsed. I

A Remarkable Inquest

mention this because it has been stated that an hour or more had elapsed before any mischief was done. It has been said, also, that all the avenues were blocked up by the police force; but such was not the fact because, in the first instance, I only took a few of my men into Calthorpe Street.'

A juror—'In your evidence you stated you received orders to march to Calthorpe Street to assist in dispersing the mob?'

Superintendent Baker—'Yes, but I found it choked up by the mob'.

Juror—'Then, when you marched your force in, you completely blocked up the street?'

Baker—'Oh no, hundreds passed me, right and left, and they were allowed to go. The first man I struck was a man who threw a brick at me.'

Juror—'By whom was the order signed that you received?'

Baker—'Sir, I object to this question as being irrelevant to this inquiry.'

A loud murmur broke out in the room and several jurors cried 'Answer! Answer!' and 'Mr Coroner, direct him to speak'.

The Coroner—'You may as well answer the question'.

Baker—'My order came from superior officers, who were the Commissioners, of course'.

Juror—'Colonel Rowan and Mr Mayne; and is it from them that the bills came?'

Baker—'Yes, we received them from the Commissioners'.

Juror—'Can anyone issue these orders besides the Commissioners?'

Baker—'No one commands them but the Secretary of State. I leave it to your superior judgment to decide who fills the highest appointment—the Commissioners or the Secretary of State.'

Juror—'By whom was the order written that you received to march to Calthorpe Street?'

At this juncture the Coroner intervened with the observation that the witness had nothing to do with the publication of the order.

Juror—'From the confusion of the mob, can you say that any of the mob stabbed the deceased; or was it done by any of his own comrades?'

Baker—'No; I certainly cannot answer that question.'

Coroner—'You cannot make him state what he does not know.'

Juror—'We wish to make him state what he does know. Did your men spring on the mob first?'

Baker—'Yes, to secure a man who carried an American flag flying. The people around were cheering and groaning in all directions.'

Juror—'What kind of a dagger was it that you say the man made a push at you with?'

Baker—'I can't say; for before the dagger reached me the truncheon of the policeman was on the head of the man who made the thrust.'

A considerable babel broke and questions were showered on the witness from all sides. The Coroner made little effort to control the situation and it was obvious that here, once more, was considerable prejudice against the police. Vested with a little brief authority, the members of the jury were determined to attack the members of the force while they had the chance. The questions were so rapid that the witness was unable to answer them. He complained that he was being treated as if he was on trial, not examined as a witness. After a semblance of order was restored the juror continued.

Juror—'Did you direct your men to seize the man who carried the American colours?'

Baker—'No, I did not, my men did it without my authority.'

Juror—'Had they a discretionary power to do so?'

Baker—'They did do so. We have in our possession all sorts of sticks and daggers—one of the latter, I believe, caused the death of the deceased. It is of French construction and is similar to one I brought from Waterloo. That dagger was found in a stable where the prisoners were secured, with a pistol, which was loaded to the muzzle. A man, who was taken before Sir Frederick Roe, acknowledged that he loaded the pistol, and that he went to the meeting to form one of the National Convention. The party who caused the dispersion of the mob amounted to sixty or ninety.'

Juror—'Did you know that any notice had been given to the people to disperse?'

Baker—'I can't answer that question; I know of none. I have

A Remarkable Inquest

been engaged in the wars, but I never saw such a set of ruffians before.'

There was a thunderous knocking on the door and when the coroner's officer opened it a Mr Prendergast, a barrister, burst in. The coroner's officer promptly seized him by the collar and attempted to turn him out. Prendergast appealed to the coroner that it was an open court and that the Court of King's Bench had so decided.

'The Court of King's Bench has decided exactly the reverse' retorted Mr Stirling.

Said Prendergast 'I have collected a great deal of information which I intend to lay before the jury'.

After further protest Prendergast suffered himself to be conducted out of the room, uttering loud remarks about injustice. Mr Stirling was right, in 1833 contemporary authority was clear that the coroner had the power to exclude, not only particular individuals, but the public generally. It was, however recommended that, as publicity assists the investigation of truth and the detection of guilt, this power should not be used without careful consideration. Nowadays, every inquest must be held in public, the only exception being when the interests of national security may be imperilled.

Mr Prendergast's interests and intentions were never disclosed. At times representatives of sectional interests try to use inquest proceedings as a platform to further a campaign or as a means of airing a personal grievance; an experienced coroner quickly detects the man with an axe to grind. Possibly Prendergast was connected with the 'Ultras' and hoped to add more fuel to an already inflammable situation.

Police Constable Henry Chance Redwood now appeared with his arm in a sling. He said that when he was about half way up Calthorpe Street he heard Sergeant Brooks exclaim 'Oh!' and saw George Fursey, now in custody, pass by carrying a flag with red and white stripes, blue in one corner with stars painted on the blue, the national flag of America. Redwood testified that he went up to Fursey and demanded that he yield up the banner. Fursey refused and Redwood grabbed hold of it. Redwood saw Fursey raise his right hand with something in it which resembled a blade about six or eight inches long, terminating in a sharp point. With the same hand he aimed a blow at the witness who put up his arm to defend himself. The instrument passed through Redwood's forearm. Redwood retained his hold on Fursey who tried to escape, still holding the dagger. Fursey ran to the left flank of the police in Calthorpe Street and was given into the custody of two other officers, whence he was taken to Busbridge's livery stables.

This evidence was of importance as establishing that Fursey was already in custody at the time when Culley was stabbed, so that Fursey cannot have been responsible for his death.

A juror—'Did you see what happened to the instrument with which you were wounded?'

Redwood—'The whole transaction did not occupy more than three minutes. I do not know what became of the instrument with which the wound was inflicted upon me, but I understand that it was found near where he was secured.'

Foreman of the jury—'Did you see any of the crowd committing a breach of the peace when you and your force came first into Calthorpe Street?'

Redwood—'I saw a man waving a banner, but I saw no other indication of a wish to break the peace.'

A juror—'Did not the people separate, and pass down on each side of the street, when the police advanced upon them?'

Redwood—'They did'.

Juror—'What orders had you from your superintendent as to taking persons into custody?'

Redwood—'I was ordered to take into custody anyone whom I saw committing a breach of the peace'.

Juror—'Do you call carrying a banner committing a breach of the peace?'

Redwood—'Not of itself, Sir, but I was told to seize any banners that I saw, if I could'.

From the back of the court Superintendent Baker stated that he could produce the dagger which was found near where Fursey was secured and which he believed could be proved to be the one with which the wound was inflicted on the witness Redwood. The dagger was produced, it had three edges and was about

A Remarkable Inquest

eight inches in length. Redwood remarked that his wound must have been caused by a three-edged weapon and offered to bare his arm so that the wound and dagger could be compared. The jury would not allow him to do this and he was ordered to withdraw.

Mr Richard Fowler, 19 Gray's Inn Lane. Sworn—

'I am an ironmonger and smith. I have a manufactory in St Pancras. About half past one o'clock on Monday I was going from my manufactory to my house for dinner, when I saw a number of persons who were assembled near this house being pushed along by the police. I was pushed by some of them, and asked where I was going to. About half past two, or near three, I was returning from my dinner when I saw a greater crowd near this house, and the police were driving men, women and children in all directions. I saw there was danger and tried to get into this house, which with great difficulty I succeeded in doing, but not until I had been struck several blows by the police. I came into this room (the inquest room upstairs) and opened the window and saw the police running by into Calthorpe Street. In a few seconds I saw the deceased returning in the direction of this house. He staggered as if he was drunk and I thought he was so. He tried to make the door, and the landlord's sister, who was standing there, made way for him, but at that moment his legs gave way under him and he fell down. I saw that he was bleeding dreadfully, and assisted him into the house. I ran to fetch a surgeon, and he came, but the man died in about eight minutes. I saw the wound and it appeared to me to have been inflicted by a four-square instrument.

A juror—'Did you see any disposition on the part of the people to kick up a disturbance on Monday?'

Fowler—'None. On the contrary, the people were running away in fright. Their only anxiety seemed to be to get away from the police unhurt. I saw no brickbats fly.'

It is already clear that this inquest was to be heavily slanted against the police by almost every witness. The jurors' questions all seem to have been directed to establishing the peaceable nature of the meeting.

George Henry Kent, of 78 Drury Lane was sworn as a witness and immediately stated 'I am a reporter but I decline to say for which paper'.

Foreman of the jury—'Why do you decline?'

Kent—'Because I think it is irrelevant to the subject of the inquiry'.

Foreman—'We don't want your opinion upon that subject. We ask you a plain question and expect a plain answer.'

Eventually the witness reluctantly admitted to being connected with the *Morning Post*. He went on that he first saw Culley in Dawson's stables at about two o'clock, before the party with the banners arrived. He heard the police ordered to fall in at about three o'clock and went with them into Calthorpe Street. Here the police party was broken into two by a cart and he saw the deceased man behind him. Kent saw Superintendent Baker struck by a stone and at this time the mob was pouring down the street into the waste land of Cold Bath Fields. There was then a great confusion. Some policemen cried 'A flag! A flag!' and rushed to the man who was carrying it. Kent did not know whether or not Culley was one of the police who rushed towards the man carrying the flag although he had the impression that he was. When he looked round again Kent saw Culley just behind him, he then lost sight of him but about eight minutes later he saw him in the yard of the Calthorpe Arms, mortally wounded.

A juror—'Did you know the deceased man well?'

Kent—'I was known to the Superintendent and all his men, and I had been in the habit of seeing the deceased every day for the last two years. I did not see the blow inflicted on him. I saw no one armed in the crowd but it was of that character that I assure you that I would not have ventured to the spot unless I had been known to Mr Baker's men, and therefore thought myself sure of the best protection they could give me. I really cannot say who were the original aggressors, and it was impossible to distinguish individual persons or acts after the affray commenced, the confusion beggaring all description.'

Police Constable Thomas Flack of C division described how he was on the right hand side of Calthorpe Street when he saw Culley emerge from a doorway, and come down the street holding his side.

A Remarkable Inquest

Culley said 'I am stabbed, I am done'. Flack then became involved in a melée with two of the mob who came from the same direction as Culley and who set upon him with some kind of weapon, he could not say what.

The Coroner—'Can you describe these men at all?'

Flack—'Yes, Sir, one was dressed in a green frock-coat with a velvet collar of the same colour, drab trousers, and white apron hanging down in front. He had light hair and a fair complexion. He carried his hat in his left hand and I had a full view of his face. He appeared to be about 5 feet 7 inches in height. The other man had on a dark snuff-coloured coat with white cravat and light waistcoat. I am not certain whether he had small-clothes or trousers on, but they were of a drab colour. He was of a very dark complexion and about 5 feet 8 inches in height.'

Foreman—'You seem to have had plenty of room and time to observe the dress and stature of these men. Pray, why did not you take them into custody?'

Flack—'We could not, Sir, there was great confusion at the time, and it happened that in that confusion I and my comrade were left behind by the rest of the force, and against such unequal odds that we had no power to apprehend the two men.'

Foreman—'Why, there were two of you, and only two of them, according to your account?'

Flack—'You don't seem to understand me, Sir, the whole mob was against us'.

Foreman—'How, then, is it that you could observe their dress and stature with so much seeming accuracy?'

This line of questioning was not pursued and the witness stood down. He was followed by the surgeon who had attended Robert Culley.

Mr Charles Everard, surgeon of 2 Tysoe Street, Wilmington Square said

'I was standing at the corner of a gateway in Gray's Inn Lane when a party of men with a banner came down the lane and turned into Calthorpe Street. Wishing to avoid the crowd I turned into Wells Street to go home but curiosity prompted me to stay to see the behaviour of the mob. While standing in a doorway at the end of Gough Street North I observed the police with uplifted staves, breaking the heads of all those who came within their reach. A number of people ran for safety into the doorway in which I was standing. A minute or two afterwards I had withdrawn into the passage of the house, when a great body of the police passed the door and then I ventured out. I saw the field below nearly covered with police and I came up Wells Street into Gray's Inn Lane, to avoid them. When within a few doors of this house I heard that a man had been wounded, and wishing of course to render any assistance in my power, I came in here and, entering the yard, found the deceased lying on his back. I examined him, and found that pulsation had nearly ceased at the wrist. I had his clothes stripped off, and found there was a punctured wound on the side which, upon examination with my finger, I ascertained had penetrated the cavity of the chest. When the head was raised a great quantity of blood issued from the mouth and I concluded from that circumstance that a great vessel had been wounded which, upon examination after death, I found to be the case. Mr Simpson, another surgeon, and I opened the body of the deceased this morning and found that a large vein had been punctured, and that a great extravasation of blood had occurred in the cavity of the chest. That was amply sufficient to cause death.'

In answer to the familiar inquiry from the jury Mr Everard said

'It was in consequence of the conduct of the policemen that I turned out of my direct road home. At the time that I witnessed the conduct on the part of the policemen that I have described, I saw no disposition on the part of the people to commit acts of violence. My opinion is that there would have been no disturbance if the police had not been there. I should not have felt in the least degree alarmed if I had not seen the police knock down indiscriminately all those who came in their way. I saw nothing like bricks or stones thrown by the mob, nor did I see any of them armed with bludgeons. In face, I saw no weapons at all in the possession of the people.'

Mr Simpson, a surgeon of Gray's Inn Lane, corroborated Mr Everard's medical evidence.

A juror then inquired of Superintendent Baker where was the captured flag and was informed that it was at Bow Street. 'You

A Remarkable Inquest

seem to have taken a great deal of pains to capture this flag and we wish to see it.'

The Superintendent undertook to bring it to the inquest the next day.

The foreman of the jury then addressed the Coroner 'Sir, it is the wish of my brethren and myself to adjourn this inquiry until to-morrow, for we feel exhausted'. It was arranged to resume the hearing at five o'clock in the afternoon of Thursday, May 16, 1833.

VIII

Some Lurid Testimony

It seems strange that inquest proceedings should have begun at five o'clock in the afternoon in a case of such public interest, the more so since the jury had complained on the previous day of being exhausted. Perhaps the Coroner wished to attend to his other business during the day, which suggests that the inquest was regarded as of secondary importance, or that he usually sat at this hour and was unwilling to depart from routine. A judicial inquiry is not best conducted by men already tired from a day's work; when the atmosphere is charged with raw emotion it is doubly important for all concerned to be fresh and alert. On the other hand, in the nineteenth century courts quite often sat on late into the night.

On Thursday, May 16th exhibits were produced before the examination of witnesses was resumed. Superintendent Baker showed a number of banners which had been taken from members of the National Union of the Working Classes. Most were attached to long poles, many of which were hinged in the middle for portability, with a metal sleeve which slid over the hinge when the pole was extended. Sharp detachable spear-heads were attached to many. The staff of the American flag which was taken from Fursey was broken in three places. There was a flag bearing the skull and crossbones and the inscription '*Liberty or Death*', a tricolour with a beehive in the centre, symbolic of industry and a banner with the words '*Equal rights and equal laws*' worked on crimson silk. Many of the flags bore the name of the class to which the particular party belonged.

Mr Baker also produced the bills calling the meeting which he said were being sold for one penny each, also the proclamation pronouncing the meeting illegal.

Some Lurid Testimony

After inspecting the exhibits the jury remarked that there did not appear to be anything very formidable about the weapons. A juryman asked whether the proclamation was signed by any person. The Coroner observed that it was merely signed 'By order of the Secretary of State'.

The hearing proper then continued with a juror asking—'Inform me, Mr Baker, if your superior officer was on the ground at the time.'

Baker—'Yes, I believe he was.'

Juror—'Was it Colonel Rowan, Mr Mayne or Lord Melbourne?'

Baker—'I do not consider that a fair question.'

Another juror—'If just, it is a fair question.'

Baker—'I saw Colonel Rowan in Gray's Inn Lane, on horseback.'

Juror—'Do you know if Lord Melbourne was on or near the spot at the time?'

Baker—'I did not see him. I do not know whether he was there.'

At this point there was another interruption. The foreman of the jury complained that the witnesses were not being provided with proper accommodation. He and the other members of the jury were prepared to subscribe for their wants and he said that he hoped that as much respect would be shown to one side as to the other.

The Coroner rather sententiously said—'I do not know what you mean by sides. You come here, and I come here, fearlessly and impartially to conduct this inquiry, without respect to anyone.'

Most of the remaining time of this session was devoted to evidence given by newspaper reporters who had attended the affray at Cold Bath Fields. The first was Mr Courtney, who represented the *Courier*. He had arrived soon after noon and mingled with the crowd, gleaning information as to the feelings of those present. Most of those present were loiterers, similar to those normally on the Fields on a Monday afternoon. None seemed desirous of participating in the meeting and the witness would not have thought that a meeting was to be held had he

The Clerkenwell Riot

not been so informed. About two o'clock so many people left that he thought there would be no meeting so he prepared to go home. Courtney saw a crowd of people in Gray's Inn Lane opposite to a stable hooting at police. He then returned along Calthorpe Street and found that the crowd on Cold Bath Fields had considerably increased.

Mr Courtney then described the arrival of the committee and the speech by Mee in the same terms as the other witnesses. The accounts of this part of the affair from various sources are almost identical. Courtney saw the banners advancing down Calthorpe Street and goes on in his own words.

'Some persons cried out "The police are coming" and three or four gentlemen connected with the press, who were with me, left the spot and went to the steps of Mr Stallwood's door. Two young women without bonnets, who appeared to be passing from one house to another, and who seemed very much frightened, begged us to open a swing gate to let them in, which we did, and they went upon the steps. Someone informed the gentleman who we were, and he admitted us upstairs to the balcony. It was not from any feeling of fear that I went there, but for the convenience of view, for I felt assured that there was not the least fear of a provocation to violence. As we passed the girls they seemed much alarmed, and I begged them not to be frightened. I afterwards saw these girls struck by the policemen of the division that came up Calthorpe Street, I believe Mr Baker's.

'When I reached the balcony, and looked down Calthorpe Street, the people had separated into two distinct lines. The middle of the street was quite clear, from the corner house where I was down to the end of the street next Gray's Inn Lane, where then a large body of the police were drawn across the street. There was not then a human being in the high road that could find footing on the pathway. Before that body of police marched their line appeared to have been broken. The middle of the street was quite clear. Whilst they halted the crowd near the place where the banner men stood gave way on each side, making a clear way to that place. At this time I saw three other large bodies of the police marching in the same way; one took the whole breadth of the street at the east end of Calthorpe Street (Gough Street). In that direction I saw a great number of persons running down towards the spot where the meeting had first been held. There was another body of police in a sort of street, with a green spot before the houses on my left as I stood on the balcony. They too made towards the spot where the meeting was held, as if it was their object strictly to close that passage. From the Bagnigge Wells Road at the prison back another very large body of police advanced in very close order, but very widely extended. I think the front rank must have consisted of sixty or seventy men. At this time the body at the end of Calthorpe Street marched on without the slightest interruption from any of the crowd. These four different bodies were moving in this manner simultaneously. The body in Calthorpe Street having halted but a short time, as I have said, marched on steadily, and without any interruption that I saw, except the disorder which the men at the end of the file occasioned by striking those of the people who stood near on the footway. Before they had reached the end of the footway I had seen several persons struck and I cried out "Shame! Shame! This looks ill; they have blocked up every passage." I said this to a person near and wrote it down at the time.

'When the division coming up Calthorpe Street reached the end of that street a rush was made by the leader of the division who stood in the centre of the front, and several of the front men rushed with him to the banner men. The crowd had given way in all directions. The division was broken by the rush made by the front rank towards the banner men and the others were in confusion. The banners were almost instantly seized, and there appeared to be a sort of scuffle there. The remainder of the division commenced striking men, women and children without distinction and without mercy. The two girls who stood on Mr Stallwood's steps were repeatedly struck. I do not say the blows were aimed at them, but they reached them. The blows were aimed, as it appeared to me, at the crowd there, standing upon and about the steps. I saw one of these girls, as she ran across the street screaming, nearly shoved down by a thrust from a staff.

'The crowd were then running in all directions and several who had gone down Gough Street then returned, as if unable to escape that way. In that direction I saw several men struck by the police as the latter made way for them to pass. I saw several policemen, as the people passed them, stoop down and strike the people on the legs until they fell. In the very beginning, almost at the instant that the banners were seized, I saw three policemen just under me, a little round the corner, strike one man who was running away, each of them several blows on the head, until he fell senseless upon the ground.'

Throughout the court room there were loud murmurs and cries of 'Shame! Shame!' Mr Courtney continued

'He fell with his head doubled under him and lay there still senseless until I left the balcony. I cried out "Shame, shame, let the man run, you rascals." One of them shook his truncheon at me and called out "You shall catch it too, you bloody bugger." I was near fainting and was obliged to go into the drawing room to recover myself.' A juror, sympathetically, 'I suppose you were frightened, Sir.'

Courtney—'I was certainly appalled at what I saw. There could not be at this time less than thirty persons within my view lying wounded on the ground. The screaming and the cries of "Shame, shame" continued and I returned to the balcony. Crowds were still running in every direction—the police pursuing and beating them and men and women falling. At a very short distance from the house where I was I saw a policeman beating a decently dressed elderly woman.'

More cries of 'Shame' from the jury.

'She was screaming violently and a gentleman who was on the balcony next to me said "Courtney, I cannot stand this. See that rascal beating that woman." He then ran downstairs and I followed him. As we were going out, some of the members of Mr Stallwood's family said "Don't go, gentlemen, they will murder you."

'When we got to the street, the whole place was nearly cleared of persons, excepting the police and the numbers who were either lying on the ground or supporting themselves against the wall, the blood streaming over their clothes. Mr Carpenter and I ran to the spot, where the policeman was still pushing the woman, and holding her at the same time. He held her by her shoulder and pushed her in her side with his truncheon at the same time. When I spoke to him he raised his truncheon and threatened to strike me. I think Mr Carpenter held his arm but I do not know for my attention was taken up by the woman. She was crying bit-

Some Lurid Testimony

terly and could scarcely walk. As I led her away she turned round repeatedly and abused the policeman. She called him a murdering villain, and other very abusive names. She was in great excitement and grief, and evidently in bodily pain. I left her with a man who came up and whom she appeared to know. In that part of the field which is near the prison there were parties of people talking and wrangling with the policemen. It was about half past three when I left the ground. I cannot identify Mr Baker or any other person as the leader.'

Courtney was of the opinion that police interference led to such rioting as there was. There was no opposition to the progress of the police and he saw no bricks, stones or missiles of any kind thrown. He said that the attack by police was wanton, brutal and without provocation. He saw no sticks in the hands of the people. The conduct of the division in Calthorpe Street was brutal and unmanly in the extreme.

Superintendent Baker, by leave of the Coroner, asked Courtney the letter of the division of police who made the attack on the colours. Courtney said he didn't know.

It is very hard to explain how Courtney, a reporter and trained observer, who had an excellent vantage point on Mr Stallwood's balcony, curiously failed to make a note of the divisional letters, which were clearly marked on the police uniform. It is difficult to understand how he failed to identify Mr Baker, who was at the head of C division in Calthorpe Street, only a few yards away from Courtney. He was not the only witness who gave clear and corroborated evidence up to the time of the arrival of police, only to produce a highly discrepant account of the events which followed, notably at the time when Culley was stabbed.

James Grant, 115 Jermyn Street, arrived at Cold Bath Fields at about one o'clock to report the meeting for the *Morning Advertiser*. His evidence of the proceedings up to the time of arrival of the police was identical with that of other witnesses. He thought that Mee did not wish to be seen by the police.

'I saw the police surround the hustings and attack the people indiscriminately in a most ferocious manner. The people ran as fast as they could and in a few minutes the ground seemed cleared. I saw a policeman strike with his staff a poor man on his back after the ground had been cleared. The man appeared to be infirm, and perfectly inoffensive; he did not seem to have taken any part in the proceedings. At the same time, in another part of the ground, some policemen were engaged in striking a woman, and the people cried "Shame, shame don't strike a woman."

'I saw nothing of the man that was killed. I saw no disposition on the part of the people to oppose the police. I saw some stones thrown on the left side of the hustings after the police made their attack. I did not see the proclamation which was issued by the National Convention, and I should not have known that the meeting was to be held if I had not seen the Government proclamation. I am of opinion that no disturbance would have taken place if the police had not interfered. I interposed to protect the old man whom the police were beating and the policeman threatened to serve me in the same way. I told him I was a reporter and he said "We want no reporters here." The attack by the police was brutal and unprovoked. They attacked persons whose appearance must have convinced them that they did not join in the views of those who called the meeting.'

The Editor of the *True Sun* newspaper was Mr William Carpenter, of Penlington Palace, Lambeth. It was unkindly said of this paper, that it came out every morning but did not shine. Mr Carpenter learned that there was to be a meeting of the committee of the National Union of the Working Classes at the Union Tavern at Bagnigge Wells Road. He arrived at the Tavern at about a quarter to two and was allowed to address the committee. He tried to dissuade them from holding the meeting which was clearly illegal. He pointed out, reasonably, that no government would sit down quietly and allow such a meeting to take place. It was then learnt that the police were in waiting in the neighbourhood and that they were supported by the military. On hearing this the committee said that they would proceed to the ground but if the police interfered they would immediately dissolve the meeting and retire. He described the subsequent events in much the same terms as Courtney and Grant. Mr Stallwood had asked them to stop crying out "Shame" because he was a magistrate of the county, but Mr Stallwood himself later joined in the outcry. He saw, he was sorry to say, several instances of persons who were prostrate on the ground being beaten by police as they lay. He mentioned other instances of violence by police officers.

Foreman of the jury—'Pray, Sir, what do you think caused this disturbance?'

Carpenter—'My decided impression was that no disturbance would have taken place but for the attack by the police. My opinion is, from the general character of the meeting, that but for the obstruction thrown in their way by the police, the people on the least alarm of the police coming would have run away. If the police had called upon the mob to disperse I am sure they would at once have separated. I saw no stones thrown by the people at all. The people were not armed with bludgeons. A gentleman seized by Mr Thomas was merely standing quietly in the street. I saw a partial struggle for the possession of the flag but I consider the attack of the police upon the people perfectly unprovoked and uncalled-for and I cried out "Shame!" very loudly.'

A witness should state facts and leave the court to draw inferences from them. An ordinary, as opposed to an expert, witness may express opinions on matters within the average man's comprehension, such as the age or condition of persons; or as to the character of a meeting alleged to be seditious. To state that people were beaten was fact; ferociously beaten, opinion. To say they were shamefully beaten is a judgment which should be left to the court and to assert that police interference led to disturbance is pure speculation. The coroner made no attempt to curb Stallwood or the three newspaper men when they made their biased comments about police conduct. It is noteworthy that three of them had been together in Stallwood's house, where there would be ample opportunity for comparing notes and that three of them were fellow members of the press.

An elegant but disdainful witness was Colonel W. L. F. de Roos, Brigade Major of the Cavalry Brigade of 3 Park Place, St James's who stated

'On Monday last, in consequence of a communication which took place between the Home Department and the Commander of the Forces I was directed to accompany Colonel Rowan, one of the Commissioners of police, taking two military officers with me, in order to obtain the earliest information and send it to the Horse Guards, and also to send to the regiment desired to be in readiness, in case the Commissioner should require military assistance in the event of the civil power not being sufficient. About half past one o'clock I went with Colonel Rowan to Busbridge's livery stables. I accompanied him into a room, the window of which looked over Gough Street, and the empty space at the back of the house of correction. From this window I saw an assemblage of people. I thought it proper to go out into the open space in order to examine the street and avenues leading to the ground. After walking round the western part of the ground I observed that about 500 people were present. I heard a man addressing them in what appeared to be a mock sermon. I returned to Busbridge's yard and took one of the military officers from there and placed him in the window of Collingridge's manufactory, from whence he could view the whole ground, and directed him to return and inform me as soon as he should see any appearance of hustings, waggons or barrows upon the ground. He came to me about a quarter before three o'clock and reported that he saw a waggon with people in it crossing the ground, and others following.

'A few minutes afterwards I saw, from the back window of the stable-yard, that the mob had increased and that a person was standing on the rail nearly opposite the end of Calthorpe Street, holding on by the lamp-post and addressing the people. There were around him several persons carrying poles and banners attached to lances. I came down into the yard and found the police formed in two bodies—one at the Gray's Inn Lane gate and the other at the Gough Street gate. A large body of the police was assembled and Colonel Rowan was addressing them. I heard him direct them to be as temperate as possible, and to endeavour to secure only such as were the leaders and offered resistance. I went out into Gough Street with one of the military leaders with me. Neither he nor I was in military costume at the time. I saw the police come out of the gateway by which I was standing. They moved with great silence and regularity towards the banners. I accompanied them to within about sixty yards of the lamp-post where the speaker was standing. I then stopped. As they went forward they appeared to me to meet with considerable resistance and a violent struggle took place for the banners. A great number of people ran past me, running down Gough Street and met with no obstruction from the police. I saw no women coming out of the crowd. As near as I could judge the resistance made to the police was overcome by them in four or five minutes. I then saw them bring into the yard several persons whom they had captured. I went into the yard and despatched an officer to the Horse Guards to say that I considered the disturbance as terminated. I examined the banners and found among them two lances, exactly corresponding with the description of those recommended in a book called *Defensive Instructions to the People*, by *Colonel Maceroni*.'

The witness produced a copy of this book which was illustrated with drawings of the weapons recommended.

'The one in question was called the "foot lance". Those captured were of the same form precisely but they had not the spike at the end. I call them in a military sense lances although they have not the blade fixed in them.'

Several members of the jury objected that since they did not have blades they could not be called lances.

Colonel de Roos—'I consider that an inkstand without a top is still an inkstand.'

Foreman—'But it would be of little use without a pen. You might as well say that a man without a head is still a man.'

An altercation developed which the coroner failed to restrain, finally, Colonel de Roos qualified his description by calling it 'part of a lance'. He stated that he had seen no women in the crowd.

Foreman—'Was there any disposition on the part of the people to create a breach of the peace?'

Colonel de Roos—'I consider the civil power was resisted when they attempted to seize the banners.'

Foreman—'But was there before the police appeared?'

Colonel de Roos—'No; because they had no one to throw at or to fight with, and they would not fight with themselves.'

Coroner—'Was any act of violence committed before the police made their appearance?'

Colonel de Roos—'Not that I saw.'

A juror—'Did you see any stones thrown?'

The Clerkenwell Riot

Colonel de Roos—'I did not see any hands raised, but I saw stones in the air, perhaps about twenty altogether.'

The inquest was then adjourned to Friday, May 17th, it then being one o'clock in the morning of Friday. As before, the hearing was to be resumed at five o'clock in the afternoon.

That morning, *The Times* contained the following paragraph

'The proceedings appeared to excite the greatest interest. The jury room was crowded to excess, and a great number of persons stood in front of the house during the whole of the evening. Several witnesses remain to be examined, and it is expected that the inquiry will occupy some days. The jury, most of whom took notes of the whole of the proceedings, appeared to take a more lively interest in the investigation than is usually envinced by persons in their situation.'

IX

Cross Purposes

By Friday, the third day of the inquest, the jury's bias against the police was clear and apparent. The coroner, who had hitherto made little attempt to control the proceedings, now began to exert a semblance of discipline. Unfortunately he was by no means the first, nor the last person in authority to mistake testy unreasonableness for firmness. Instead of pulling together to ascertain the true circumstances of Culley's death coroner and jury became increasingly at cross-purposes.

After the court opened a youth stepped forward and said he wanted to give evidence. The coroner asked what he knew about the deceased man's death and he replied that he was in Calthorpe Street when the police made their attack. The coroner pointed out that several witnesses had already spoken of the events in Calthorpe Street which had nothing to do with Culley's death. What had the jury to do with the conduct of the police? That must be reserved for another tribunal, and the simple question which the jury had to decide was, what caused the death of the deceased? This was a perfectly correct statement of the function of the coroner's inquest.

Foreman of the jury—'I beg your pardon, Sir. The summons which we received, and a copy of which I now hold in my hand, enjoins us "to inquire, on His Majesty's behalf, touching the death of the deceased" and also contains this important intimation—"and further, to do and execute such other matters and things as shall be then and there given you in charge".'

Coroner—'But it is not necessary for you to inquire as to the conduct of the police after the man was killed.'

Foreman—'But if the witnesses that you object to are examined, circumstances may come out which we are anxious to investigate. As tradesmen, we are not anxious to waste our time, and we entered on this inquiry purely with a spirit of justice.'

Coroner—'What can the man state who tendered his evidence? In answer to my question, he said he knew nothing of the death of the deceased.'

Foreman—'We are anxious that he should be examined, to see if he does know anything.'

Coroner—'Why, he will probably tell you that he saw the meeting and the flags taken from the people. Is it to be supposed that when the men with the flags made a resistance, the police, who had received directions to clear the ground, would not resort to violence? However, gentlemen, let the young man be examined.'

Foreman—'We only wish to have the liberty of calling him, we don't wish to examine him now.'

Coroner—'I will examine him when I please. It is for me to decide what witnesses shall be examined.'

Foreman—'Previous to the commencement of the proceedings the jury are anxious that your attention should be directed to a circumstance which has come to their knowledge. They have heard that many persons who received wounds on the day of the meeting are fearful to come forward. The jury are not aware why they entertain these feelings, and are therefore anxious that the coroner should inform them that there is no foundation for their fears.'

Coroner—'I cannot protect them. They must be conscious that what they state is nothing but the truth.'

Foreman—'Persons who have been beaten are fearful of coming forward, we are convinced that unless their evidence is heard the course of justice will be impeded.'

Coroner—'If the parties know anything of the affair and choose to give evidence, they shall be safe in coming here and returning. Beyond that I cannot protect them.'

The first witness to be examined on Friday, May 17, 1833 was a middle-aged clerk named John Todd, who lived in West Street, Smithfield. He was shaky, his arm was in a sling and he spoke almost in a whisper, which he attributed to exhaustion from the wounds which he had received. He said that he was a stranger to London and that he went to the meeting out of curiosity, having seen the notices forbidding it. He saw a number of persons with banners which he thought rather ludicrous. Todd remained in Gough Street and between two and three o'clock a body of police came from a nearby street and formed in two lines. Todd then decided it was time to leave the meeting and attempted to withdraw when the police began to use their batons on him and on some women. Todd begged and begged for mercy but in vain, he was belaboured and received a blow on the back of his neck, which, he said, injured him severely. While he was asking for mercy he got another blow on the back and, on raising his arm to protect himself he was struck just above the wrist.

Todd was taken to a surgeon who diagnosed a fractured arm and sent him to St Bartholomew's Hospital, where the bone was set. 'The night before last I had a return of epilepsy, which I laboured under some years ago, but I consider that the blow on the back of my head was the cause of the return of that complaint. From the fear of the return of epilepsy I cannot pursue my usual avocations and I must therefore return to my parish.'

Todd told the jury he did not hear the Riot Act read. So far from being a breach of the peace he considered it a silly ridiculous meeting not worth the attention of the magistracy. He was sure there would have been no breach of the peace if the police had not attacked the people. When the police struck him they had used shameful language and damned him. Todd had not seen a policeman fall, nor stones thrown. The crowd had no bludgeons, they were an inoffensive set of persons and it was a disgrace for any man to raise his hand to them.

There was a further interruption by the jury who sought to select those witnesses which its members wished to examine. While a coroner is anxious to see that justice is done and that a proper regard is had to those who may assist the inquiry, the summoning of witnesses and the general conduct of the case is his responsibility, and the jury should not have been allowed to interfere to the extent that they did in the Culley inquest.

Juror—'Sir, I request that a young girl who was on the ground and saw the policeman stabbed should be called. I regret to observe that there has been a great deal of party feeling mixed up with this inquiry but, as this girl is only thirteen or fourteen years of age, it is not to be supposed that she would be influenced by those feelings which influence the minds of other people.'

Foreman—'I wish to have those persons examined who are in a dangerous state.'

Juror—'I agree that we should not mix up with this inquiry anything that occurred after the man was killed and I repeat that we should hear that evidence which immediately relates to that question.'

Coroner—'A number of gentlemen who are on duty at the Horse Guards wish to be examined.'

Truth, compassion, social status—which was to prevail?

Charles Wheeler, an official of the Society for Suppressing Cruelty to Animals said he was previously employed in Galway to prevent bull-baiting. He had been on duty in Smithfield and was walking home with his wife. Passing the end of Calthorpe Street he saw the police driving the people up the street, beating everyone in reach.

'One young man was struck across the eye by a truncheon. I said to my wife I was not aware of the crowd and that we would go home another way. I accordingly went round the street into the Bagnigge Wells Road. In passing along the road I again saw the young man who was struck in Calthorpe Street; his eye was then bleeding. I said, "You have suffered severely, the man belongs to the H division and you can go tomorrow and pick him out." While I was in conversation I heard several women, who came from an aperture in the field, screaming. They were followed in the rear by a number of policemen of A division. I was forced from the pavement into the road by the crowd. I turned round to look for my wife, who had just then separated from me, when I saw a policeman—A 32—with a truncheon in his hand and his arm uplifted take a deliberate aim at me and hit me on the head. I fell from the violence of the blow and I became senseless. I had no recollection of anything that occurred till I found myself in the shop of a medical gentleman. My clothes were literally soaked with blood, which ran down into my boots and stockings.'

Here Wheeler, whose head was bandaged and who appeared very ill, produced the clothes which he wore on the day of the affray. They were saturated with blood and their exhibition was the cause for a murmur of horror which went through the room. There was hissing and cries of 'Dreadful! Shame! Scandalous!'

The witness continued—'I was told afterwards by a person who witnessed the transaction that I was kicked while I was down, and I believe such to be the fact, because I found my shoulders and sides very sore and much bruised.'

Coroner—'Did you form one of the meeting?'

Wheeler—'No, Sir, I never attend political meetings. I endeavoured as much as possible to avoid the crowd, and it was by mere accident that I was there. I have been under medical care ever since.'

There was a movement in the room and a man, unidentified, handed a note addressed to the foreman of the jury. The Coroner noticed this movement and remarked that it was extremely improper to attempt to communicate with any of the jury, who were on oath to judge of the case from the evidence which was regularly put before them. The note was returned unopened and the man who had passed it up was removed by order of the coroner.

Thomas Middleton Biddulph, sworn,—'I am an officer in the first Regiment of Life Guards. I was ordered on the 13th inst., last Monday, to come here and place myself under orders of Colonel de Roos. I came here and went to the White Horse Yard livery stables (Busbridge's stables). About one hour after I came, at about three o'clock, a large reinforcement of police came in. They were formed and directly afterwards ordered to proceed out. Some went out from a door behind the yard. I went out also and immediately afterwards saw several persons seized. I did not see anyone hurt by the police. The orders that I heard issued immediately before they went out were that they should not hurt anybody if they could help it, or words to that effect. I remained out about five minutes. I heard one of the crowd who was brought into the yard between two policemen say that, although they had him, it would cost some of the policemen their lives.'

Foreman—'You say you were ordered here; pray, by whom?'

Biddulph—'I received the order from the Horse Guards.'

Foreman—'By whom was the order signed?'

Biddulph—'I received an order verbally from Colonel Lygon.'

Foreman—'Oh! Colonel Lygon was it? But from whom did the order first emanate?'

Biddulph—'I do not know. Colonel Lygon had no doubt received directions and he sent the order to me.'

Foreman—'Did you see any of the people commit a breach of the peace, or do anything to deserve being taken up?'

Biddulph—'I did not see them do anything in particular. I saw no stones thrown. I saw no women in the crowd. I did not see the crowd do anything that was illegal unless their assembling there was unlawful. I did not see the people make any resistance to the police. I saw one man with a bludgeon.'

Thomas Bulkeley, another officer from the first Regiment of Life Guards, stationed at Regent's Park Barracks said—

'I received orders to be in attendance at Busbridge's livery stables in Gray's Inn Lane on Monday last and came there about two o'clock. I received orders to go to Collingridge's manufactory in Gough Street and to report if I saw any procession or waggon arrive. I had been there about a quarter of an hour when a waggon arrived with some persons in it, one of whom addressed the assembled people. I immediately returned to the stables and reported the arrival of the waggon. There were then about fifty persons present besides those in the waggon. A short time after a procession passed by in Gray's Inn Lane, accompanied by a number of persons, some of whom were carrying banners. The police then received orders from Colonel Rowan to turn out, and before they marched he directed them not to use any unnecessary violence. They marched up Gough Street. I did not see them use any violence, on the contrary, every person had an opportunity of escaping who chose to do so. I returned in a short time to the stables, where I saw several prisoners brought in, only one of whom showed any mark of violence. I heard one of the prisoners say "You have taken a few of us. You may depend upon it some of you (meaning the police) will lose your lives." I was despatched to the Horse Guards in about five minutes from the time that the police marched out to report that the mob was dispersed.'

In answer to the jury Biddulph said he saw no riot, nor did he see a policeman strike any of the crowd, nor any of the crowd strike a member of the police. Biddulph saw no stones thrown, nor any breach of the peace committed. No magistrate warned the crowd or read out the Riot Act. The police did not extend quite the whole width of the street because he saw many persons coming down each side of the street to go away. He had seen the long staves, which he called lances, but they had no blades with them. He heard people hissing at the police and also a lot of cheering.

The next witness was far more relevant to the subject of the inquest. She was a rather undernourished girl of fourteen who lived at 45 George Street, Bagnigge Wells Road. Giving her name as Mary Ann Perkins she said 'On Monday last I was standing in a court near the Union public house, Bagnigge Wells. I saw a man stab a policeman and make his escape over some railings. I cannot say what kind of a man he was. He had blue trousers but I cannot tell whether he had a black or a blue coat. He stabbed the policeman with something which he took out of a walking stick. The policeman struck him over the shoulder before he stabbed him. He struck him with his staff and then the man drew his dagger out and struck him. There were several policemen there at the time, some sitting down and others standing up. None of the others struck him. When he ran away they ran after him. He left the stick behind him. I do not know where he went to when he leaped the palings. I ran away frightened.'

Mary Perkins said the man who stabbed the policeman was dressed like a working man, but looked respectable. On the face of things it seems unlikely that, if her testimony was true, she could have witnessed the stabbing of Culley, who must have been more than a hundred yards away in Calthorpe Street when he received the fatal wound.

Now came another interruption by the self-important Nathaniel Stallwood, which was treated with remarkable equanimity by the coroner. Stallwood said 'Sir, I beg leave to correct one word in the evidence I gave on Wednesday. I then stated that Mr Thomas, the Superintendent of Police, called me a scoundrel. The term he used was "fellow", and not scoundrel. Another thing I wish to mention, Sir, is that it was stated in the newspapers that I said I saw 300 policemen, whereas I said, distinctly, that I saw 1500.' Mr Stallwood said, with great warmth and considerable violence of manner.

The Clerkenwell Riot

'I have been grossly vilified in *The Times*, they stated that I was dismissed from the commission of the peace. I certainly was struck off but only because I did my best to upset the select vestry of St Pancras. I was shamefully treated and His Grace the Duke of Portland refused to let me see the evidence upon which I was removed.'

'The people who come here' shouted Mr Stallwood in tones of thunder 'from *The Times* ought to speak the truth or else they should be expelled; that's what I think'. This was a most imprudent speech and, had Stallwood seen the covered smirks of the reporters and the messenger boys hurrying from the room with notes he would have repented of it before he did. The man who complains of press treatment must be very sure of his ground. Mr Stirling remarked that if Mr Stallwood had anything to complain of the remedies of the law were open to him.

Thomas Arnold, whose head was bandaged, testified to being beaten by police. He said he was so bad that he was unable to stoop nor go to work. He said that the police spat in their hands before they used their truncheons, which meant that they intended violence.

The next witness was a man of substance whose evidence seemed more reliable. He was Mr William Henry Goore, a solicitor, of Broadway in Worcestershire. He had met the procession of the National Union of the Working Classes going down Gray's Inn Lane and had found out that they were going to Cold Bath Fields. He had pointed out that the Secretary of State had declared the meeting illegal, but they said the proclamation was neither effective nor legal because it was not signed by Lord Melbourne. When Mr Goore pointed out that Government had the power to issue such a proclamation the members of the procession replied 'We are going in no way to disturb the Government, nor the peace of the country; our only object is that of entering into a resolution and on that resolution grounding a petition to Parliament seeking those remedies which have been denied by the present ministers to the people as to the assessed taxes.'

Said Mr Goore

'I told them to be guarded in their conduct at the place of meeting, well convinced from what I heard that the police were lying in ambush close to the place where they intended to hold the meeting. After I had given them that counsel I walked by the side of them till they approached the spot destined for the meeting. I thought it good generalship to keep thirty or forty yards distant from where the speaker and others had congregated together.'

Mr Goore went on to describe Mee's speech and the arrival of the police just as the other witnesses had done.

'The police formed themselves in rank and file, breasting the whole width of the street, and rendering it impossible for anybody to pass. I at that time, without any cause or provocation, not being mixed with the crowd, being forty yards from them, was knocked down by the police with their bludgeons. I made some remonstrance with the man who first struck me and his reply was "Damn you, I'll knock you to the devil if you say another word". Perhaps forty or fifty policemen walked over me, treading on and bruising various parts of my body before I could recover strength to raise myself from the ground. A gentleman about four yards from me was leaning against the palisades; he had received two cuts in the arm, one of which had broken the limb. I requested his name, and he said "My servant is not far off with my gig, which I left in his care while I came from motives of curiosity to see the meeting. I will not give my name, but I've said I am a person of some respectability and if my name is disclosed Government may say that I was in some way concerned with getting up the meeting". I assisted him towards his gig, and before I left him I asked him if the police desired him to move away, or did he commit any violence. He replied, neither. Immediately after that a man near me was cut down by a policeman's staff, and he received a wound in his skull of the length of my finger. I rendered him—incapable as I was—every assistance. Feeling exceedingly anxious that the thing should be made public, I went with the man to the *True Sun* office, giving him a note, in order that the circumstances should be made known. I saw no breach of the peace committed by those handful of boys who formed the principal part of the meeting. The whole of the avenues were blocked up; there was no possibility or chance of any man escaping. I do, upon my oath, say that if the police had not interfered there would have been no disturbance.'

The Clerkenwell Riot

A juror—'If you had had a stick with you, would you have resented the blow?'

Goore—'Certainly, I would have cut off the head of the man who gave it!'

Juror—'If you had had a knife, would you have used it?'

Goore—'Certainly, I should have considered myself justified in resisting such a murderous attack.'

Was Goore's presence at the meeting so innocent? It is strange to contemplate the behaviour of a respectable solicitor from a small Cotswold village who, quite by chance, comes upon a procession of working men, parleys with them and then joins in their march. Who was the mysterious stranger who spoke of the gig? Goore only went with him 'towards' the gig, he never saw this conveyance. Why was Goore, a countryman, so vehement against the police? Why would the *True Sun* be so much in the forefront of his mind?

William Robinson, of 5 Bolton Place, Margaret Street, Spa Fields, said

'I am a surgical instrument maker. I was on the spot when the deceased was stabbed. I was returning from Berners Street and when I arrived in Calthorpe Street I saw the police advancing in a body. I saw the meeting and heard Mr Lee propose Mr Mee as Chairman, and the latter exhorted the people to be quiet and orderly. The police then came up and halted within three or four yards of the people. They then rushed upon the people whom they knocked down one by one as they came within their reach. I was knocked down by a blow on the temple, the marks of which you can see now, and while down I was beaten without mercy by several policemen for about five minutes, until their attention was called to a man and woman whom they attacked and knocked down. I met Mr Charles Wheeler who said he had the number of the policeman who had knocked me down. Three policemen then rushed upon Mr Wheeler and beat him severely.

'Wheeler was then taken to a surgeon's and his wounds were dressed. While I was bleeding several policemen passed me and some of them said, with a savage expresion of countenance "I say, old fellow, we didn't come out for nothing". I saw at one time upwards of fifty persons wounded and bleeding. The police took no notice of those who were wounded. I think the police were drunk, for their countenances indicated as much.'

After William Robinson had withdrawn the coroner said to the jury

'Really, gentlemen, I don't know what we are to have proved next. The last witness has found out that the police were drunk. This is rather an extraordinary discovery, for of all the witnesses who have been previously examined not one of them has said a word about their being drunk.'

Foreman—'No, Sir, because the question was never asked. We could hardly suppose that peace officers could be drunk.'

After the inquest had been readjourned there was talk in the jury room. It was stated, without very good authority, that ninety-six witnesses remained to be examined, including Lord Melbourne, Colonel Rowan and Mr Mayne. The jury expressed strong determination to investigate the whole affair down to the last detail.

Poor Culley was buried on the afternoon of Friday, May 17, 1833, four days after he was stabbed to death. About 200 of his police comrades attended the funeral at St Anne's, Soho. When the mourners reached the church they were met by a howling mob of about 300 persons, who jeered and booed at the police and crudely referred to the affray four days before. Even in the presence of death there was no respect, nothing but hatred. Culley, who was buried in St Anne's burial ground, had been married two years. He had no children but his wife was far advanced in pregnancy. Between £40 and £50 had already been subscribed for the relief of his widow and it was anticipated that she would receive a Government pension.

X

An Interlude. Mr Stallwood's Nemesis

Nemesis overtook Mr Stallwood on Monday, May 20th in the shape of a column in *The Times*.

MR STALLWOOD

'We have received the following documents which we think will explain the grounds of that rumour to which we alluded on Friday.

'Middlesex—These are to certify that at the general quarter sessions of the peace of our late Sovereign Lord the King George IV holden in and for the county of Middlesex at the Sessions House for the said county by adjournment on Monday, the 22nd October in the second year of the reign of our late Sovereign Lord George IV by grace of God of the United Kingdom of Great Britain and Ireland, Defender of the Faith. Nathaniel Stallwood, late of the Parish of St Pancras in the said county, labourer, and Jeremiah Sullivan, late of the same Parish, labourer, were according to due form of law severally convicted on an indictment against them for assaulting, beating and wounding John Jones the younger on the 10th day of July 1821; and these are further to certify that the said Nathaniel Stallwood, Thomas Smith and Jeremiah Sullivan were then and there for the said offence sentenced as follows—that is to say, the said Nathaniel Stallwood to pay a fine of £20 with liberty to speak to the prosecutor, which fine was afterwards at the same session remitted to one shilling. The said Thomas Smith to pay a fine of 6s 8d and the said Jeremiah Sullivan to be imprisoned in the House of Correction in this county for one month.
Dated the 12th day of May 1821.
   H. C. SELBY, Clerk of the Peace.'

An Interlude. Mr Stallwood's Nemesis

Palace Court
11 Manchester Square
May 11th 1831

'*George Johnston, plaintiff: and Nathaniel Stallwood and James Hope, defendants.*

'I hereby certify that the above cause was tried on Friday, the 18th day of May 1827, that a verdict was given for the plaintiff with £80 damages.

Dated this 14th day of May 1831
J. C. HEWLETT, Deputy Prothonotary.'

'Gentlemen,
The circumstances of the recent transaction with Mr Nathaniel Stallwood are these:— Mr Stallwood was assessed for premises in Gough Street to Lady Day 1830. Mr Stallwood having attended before the magistrates to show cause against payment of rates stated that the premises were empty and upon his offering to verify his statement upon oath the magistrates, without proceeding to administer the oath (although the book was tendered and about to be received by Mr Stallwood) remitted the amount of the rate.

'It subsequently appearing that, notwithstanding Mr Stallwood's statement, the premises were occupied and had produced a considerable rental, the vestry requested the circumstances to be again investigated by the magistrates and it then appeared that Mr Stallwood was incorrect, he was ordered to pay the amount, but refusing to do so, a warrant of distress was issued against him, and the sum distrained for upon which distraint I gave Mr Stallwood a receipt. I subsequently demanded rates to Michaelmas 1830. Mr Stallwood refused to pay it on the grounds that he was not properly assessed. He was thereupon again threatened with process for that rate. On a communication with him it turned out that he claimed a discharge from the rate to Michaelmas upon the former receipt given by me for the Lady Day rate.

'Upon the production of the receipt it appeared that I had inadvertently given him a printed Michaelmas receipt without altering the word "Michaelmas" to "Lady Day", as I ought to have done (not having any of the Lady Day receipts in my possession); and Mr Stallwood therefore contended that holding a receipt to Michaelmas, he was discharged. I explained that the variation of the amount of the two rates was sufficient evidence of the last one not having been paid, even if he himself was not aware of the fact. He still contended for his discharge under the receipt that I had erroneously given, and tendered the amount of the other rates, which I offered to take, and did take, on account. He gave me a check for the amount on the Bank of England and I sent him receipts according to my understanding of the matter. Upon this he discharged his check, notwithstanding he held the receipts.

'I therefore felt it necessary, under the sanction of my legal adviser, to proceed against him at law; but Mr Stallwood, no doubt finding it impossible to offer any defence, paid the money to my solicitor.

'I have given a detail of the circumstances as correctly and concisely as possible.

> I have the honour to be, gentlemen,
> Your most obedient servant,
> J. WORRELL.

To the magistrates of St Pancras.'

This letter was considered at a meeting of the vestry of St Pancras on June 1, 1831. Mr Richard Winstanley, churchwarden, was in the chair and no fewer than fifty-two vestrymen were present. The justices present stated that they felt an insurmountable difficulty in acting with Mr Stallwood, which is understandable in view of the contents of the letter from Mr Worrell, who was the official responsible for collection of rates. There can be little doubt that this was only the tip of an iceberg of dubious transactions and awkward behaviour. After discussion it was resolved:—

'That the vestrymen be summoned for the next vestry to take into consideration the difficulty in which the vestry is placed, in consequence of a communication to the magistrates respecting the recovery of the poor rates and to consider the necessary measures to be adopted for relieving the Parish from such difficulties.'

An Interlude. Mr Stallwood's Nemesis

The meeting further resolved that:—

'That an extract from the minutes of the last meeting be forwarded to His Grace the Lord Lieutenant of the County accompanied by a document respectfully informing His Grace of the opinion of this vestry as to the inconveniences likely to result to the parish by the appointment of Mr Stallwood, and that a deputation of three of the vestry will have the honour to wait upon His Grace to afford him such further information upon the subject as His Grace will be pleased to require.'

There is no further information as to the peccadilloes of Mr Stallwood at this time but eighteen months later the vestry again assembled on January 7, 1833 to hear the case of a Mrs Walker, formerly of 19 Calthorpe Street. *The Times* reported as follows:—

'Mr Worrell, one of the collectors being in attendance, was called in and he then requested the vestry to hear the case. Mr Stallwood was present but took no active part in the proceedings. Mrs Elizabeth Walker, late of 19 Calthorpe Street had been rated as a defaulter for the rate to Michaelmas Last. Upon inquiry it was stated that the rate had been paid. The landlord of the house is Mr Stallwood, a vestryman. It was resolved that a committee of nine vestrymen be appointed to investigate the subject.'

A fortnight later the committee of nine reported back to the vestry meeting. Thomas Russell, churchwarden, was in the chair and sixty-two vestrymen of St Pancras were present. The committee stated:—

'That they find Mr Nathaniel Stallwood, one of the vestrymen of this Parish, is the landlord of the house and several others in Calthorpe Street; that for a considerable period previously to the rate which was laid for services of the poor up to Michaelmas it was his wish to be individually rated for such houses as he had let to tenants at rents including the rates and that the tenants should not be rated.

'That some time previously to such rate being made Mr Stallwood directed Mr Worrell, the collector, to have his tenants rated instead of himself, but not to demand the rates of them, he engaging to continue to pay them.

'On about the 18th of December last Mr Worrell called on Mr Stallwood for the rates on which Mr Stallwood, in his presence, made out a list of tenants for whom he would pay, but from that list he omitted the house No 19 Calthorpe Street, which omission was not discovered by Mr Worrell until he was entering the money received in the books. That a few days afterwards Mr Worrell claimed the rate due on the house in question of Mr Stallwood, who refused to pay it, saying that his tenant Mrs Walker had gone away without paying her rent and he knew not where to find her. In consequence thereof Mr Worrell wrote off the rate as "bad and gone".

'In the course of subsequent inquiries he discovered that Mr Snowden, of the Haymarket, the son-in-law of Mrs Walker, acted as her agent, who had not only paid the rate and rents due at Michaelmas but those likewise due at Christmas. The latter was paid by Mr Snowden to Mr Stallwood, for which his receipt was produced.

'That explanation being demanded in vestry on 7th inst from Mr Stallwood, he publicly acknowledged having received the Michaelmas rate previously to his refusal to pay it to Mr Worrell.

'That so far from Mrs Walker having left Mr Stallwood's premises clandestinely, as Mr Stallwood stated to Mr Worrell, he also acknowledged in vestry that he was aware that Mrs Walker had proceeded to Liverpool, but to what exact spot he knew not.

'It is worthy of remark that the Christmas rate and rent were paid to Mr Stallwood, as appears on his own receipt, two days after Christmas day, say on the 27th of December.

'That the result of the investigation leads your committee to consider the transactor to be highly dishonourable, disreputable to the individual and derogatory to the character of a vestryman.

'Your committee feel it their duty to state that they consider Mr Stallwood an unfit person to be a member of the vestry of St Pancras, or to have any control whatsoever in the administration of parochial affairs.'

It was resolved that the report of the committee be approved and agreed to.

This meant that Mr Stallwood was removed from the magis-

An Interlude. Mr Stallwood's Nemesis

tracy only four months before the Cold Bath Fields affray. His character and methods of conducting business must have been well known in St Pancras, so the effrontery of his behaviour at the inquest verged on the mentally abnormal. The Lord Lieutenant of Middlesex was the Duke of Portland, to whom Stallwood referred in court on Friday, May 17, 1833.

XI

The Fourth Day of the Inquest

The proceedings at the Calthorpe Arms started on Monday, May 20th shortly after eleven o'clock in the morning. Mr John Jeffery, of Well Street, Gray's Inn Lane, a cabinet maker, was working in a second floor front room in Calthorpe Street, four doors down from Mr Stallwood's, so that he had a good view of the affray. He described the arrival of the hustings, Mee's speech and heard the cry 'take the tops off the spears' and a voice call 'as we would the King's head'. He heard Mee exhort the crowd to be peaceable. Jeffery saw the man carrying the American flag and saw a man in a frock coat point to the flag and shout 'Be firm, liberty or death, down with the police.'

Jeffery saw a scuffle between the man carrying the American flag and a police officer. The man thrust repeatedly at the police officer with the flag pole, struck him on the breast and knocked him down, continuing to strike him as hard as he could. Another policeman came up and struck the man a violent blow on the head, which knocked his hat off and broke the hat. The flag bearer then let go of the flag and ran in a stooping position with his hands across the back of his head, pursued by the officers. The policeman who had been in the conflict walked in a staggering way towards another police division which was then approaching. Another police officer broke the flagpole into three pieces and threw them away.

After this Jeffery went round to his home in Well Street, found that all was in order and returned to the house in Calthorpe Street where he was working. He heard Mr Stallwood angrily haranguing the crowd. He heard Stallwood say that he was a county magistrate; Jeffery, knowing the contrary, almost doubted

The Fourth Day of the Inquest

his own ears. He said from that moment the people again collected beneath Stallwood's balcony, taking courage, as Jeffery presumed, from what Mr Stallwood said.

Foreman of the jury—'Do you admit this as evidence, Mr Coroner, the witness is stating something that he presumed?'

Coroner—'It certainly is not evidence.'

Witness—'The policemen formed again, and the word "forward" was given, and the moment the police moved the people dispersed and the police came back again to the same spot.'

Foreman—'Earlier in your evidence you stated that the man who addressed the people spoke in language calculated to excite the worst passions. Did you hear him exhort the people to keep the peace?'

Jeffery—'I did. He said "be peaceable, for the spies of the Government are about you. Be peaceable but firm"!'

Foreman—'And you call that language calculated to excite the worst passions?'

Jeffery—'I do. There are two ways of saying a thing, you know, Sir.'

Another juror remarked 'I saw a number of spearheads upon the flagstaffs. Almost all the flagstaffs had spears fixed into the heads of them.'

Foreman—'You have given an elaborate description of the scuffle between the flag-bearer and the policeman. Pray, how long did it occupy?'

Jeffery—'About two minutes—please do not try to confuse me.'

Foreman—'I have no desire to confuse you, I only wish to get at the truth. You say it was not a wound that the flag-bearer received, but a scratch. Will you be good enough to give us your definition of a wound?'

Jeffery—'By a scratch I mean when only the skin is divided, a wound is when the weapon has penetrated into the flesh. There was very little blood on this occasion.'

Foreman—'Did the police or the people make the first attack?'

Jeffery—'As far as pressing on the people can be called an attack, the attack certainly was commenced by the police.'

A juror—'Did you see any stones thrown?'

Jeffery—'I did not.'

The Clerkenwell Riot

Juror—'Did you see any of the people armed with bludgeons?'

Jeffery—'The political people had long staves, but I saw no bludgeons. By the political people I mean those who took the leading part in the meeting. I saw no one wounded but the man who was scratched. I saw a number of sticks in the crowd but no bludgeons. I have no desire to convert a stick into a bludgeon.'

Juror—'Did the flag-bearer run away at a fast rate?'

Jeffery—'He did.'

Juror—'How could he run fast with his hands on his head in a stooping position?'

Jeffery—'Why, I could run fast for a short distance in such a position.'

Coroner—'Do you know whether the policeman who was thrust at with the flagstaff by the flag-bearer, as you have already described, was the same man who was killed?'

Jeffery—'I do not know.'

Juror—'When the policeman went away in a staggering position, did you perceive if he was wounded?'

Jeffery—'I could not observe it, he went away with his hand placed on his left breast.'

Juror—'How far from Gray's Inn Lane was it that this occurred?'

Jeffery—'About twenty-five yards from the field end.'

Juror—'Did you observe that the spear with which the man was struck or poked had on it a spear head?'

Jeffery—'I did not; and I beg to observe that the assault on the man was committed by the ground end of the spear, not the flag end, as the man who carried the spear had the flag furled round the pole and it was placed under his arm. I do not know which end was first used.'

Juror—'You have not told us what the chairman said to the meeting.'

Jeffery—'He said "If I get into trouble, will you support my wife and family?".'

Juror—'Did you see the police strike the people?'

Jeffery—'I certainly did not. I saw the police push the people.'

Juror—'If they did so when dispersing the crowd, must you have seen it from the place where you stood?'

Jeffery—'Certainly I must have seen it. I saw the people dispersing over the field, which they had ample room to do. I think if I had been among the crowd on the open space I could have got away.'

Juror—'Did you see any stones thrown in the direction of Gough Street from the field?'

Jeffery—'I saw no stones thrown.'

Juror—'Had the policeman hold of the flag-staff at the time the thrust was made at him?'

Jeffery—'Yes, and right manfully he fought.'

Juror—'Do you think there would have been any disturbance if the police had not come up?'

Jeffery—'I do not think such a question ought to be put to me; how is it possible for me to give such an opinion?'

Juror—'Did you see any acts of violence committed by the people previous to the arrival of the police?'

Jeffery—'No, the proceedings had not occupied ten minutes when the people came up.'

Juror—'In the scuffle that took place between the policeman and the man with the pole, did you observe that the man with the pole stooped down, as if to stab the policeman?'

Jeffery—'I did not; I should think he did not do so; if he had, he must have lost his hold of the pole, and which he was struggling to keep possession of.'

Foreman—'Have you been requested to come here?'

Jeffery—'No, I came voluntarily, I told the officer I would attend. I am a housekeeper in the neighbourhood, and have property in it. I feel the expense of the police as much as any man, but I also feel the necessity of security.'

Jeffery's evidence was of importance, if in a negative way. He was clearly a reliable, honest witness who weighed his words and who would not be drawn to go beyond what he had seen. He described a tussle between a man bearing an American flag and two police officers. Fursey had carried such a flag and its staff was produced in Court, broken in three pieces as described by Jeffery. The details of the struggle differ from the accounts given by Sergeant Brooks and P.C. Redwood, who were concerned, but it must be remembered that Jeffery was looking down on the scene from a second storey window. The policeman who had staggered towards the approaching support division could have been Sergeant Brooks. As this incident took place while Culley was in the support division it happened before he was stabbed. Fursey was immediately taken in custody when the flag was seized so Jeffery's evidence weighs heavily in favour of Fursey's innocence of Culley's death.

Joseph Saddler Thomas, Superintendent, F Division, was next examined, he said:—

'I received orders to assemble at the station house in Bow Street 100 constables, ten sergeants and two inspectors with myself and take them to the riding school in Gray's Inn Lane by one o'clock in the day, where they were to remain for further orders. We assembled at the station house previous to leaving, which I addressed a few words to the men on the nature of the business they were to be engaged in. My words, as near as I can recollect, were to this effect:—"Now, men you are going out under circumstances which may possibly prove serious. I therefore have to entreat that you will pay particular attention to what I am saying. Circumstances may possibly bring you into collision with the people—I hope that will not be the case, but should it unhappily turn out so, recollect that the orders of the Commissioners are, at all times, and under all circumstances, to execute your instructions with fidelity and firmness, but also with humanity. Don't forget, men, that these are your own countrymen you are going among; therefore I have to implore you to act with moderation and forbearance. Don't suffer yourselves to be ill-treated but, at the same time, don't use your staves unnecessarily, but as a last resort and as a measure of self-defence."

'Those were my observations, nearly word for word, which I addressed to the men and which I conceived to be the wishes of the Commissioners. We then proceeded to Gray's Inn Lane; I think I got my division in the riding school about a quarter past one. We remained till a quarter past three when a sergeant of A division came running down Gray's Inn Lane, calling to us to turn out. There were parties of four divisions in the riding school at that time. We had previously received an intimation that in case we were wanted we should march in certain order; the C first, then E and F and lastly S. We left the riding school in that order and, the doorway being narrow, it took some time for us to clear out. When we got into the road we formed into columns of twenty-five.

The Fourth Day of the Inquest

'We then proceeded into Calthorpe Street. By the time I had got with my division into Calthorpe Street I found the meeting had been dispersed. As soon as I had got in and halted my men, a respectable-looking man informed me that one of my own men had been stabbed. I came round to this house where I saw a man whom I knew perfectly well bleeding, and apparently dying. I gave some necessary instructions as to supporting his head and allowing him to have all the air he could. I then went into Well Street and passed round Mr Stallwood's house, where I found a crowd of about a dozen persons under Mr Stallwood's balcony. Mr Stallwood was calling out in a very loud and vehement way that the police had acted in a very disgraceful manner; that they had acted illegally; that the people were not to blame, and that the police had acted illegally as the Riot Act had not been read. Some persons under the balcony threatened vengeance against the police. Two persons in particular were pointed out to me as having made use of some deadly threats. I called to Mr Stallwood repeatedly and begged him to desist.'

At this point another of the frequent interruptions which punctuated these ill-controlled proceedings took place. The street outside the Calthorpe Arms was packed with onlookers and a roar of applause and cheering now broke out, causing Superintendent Thomas to pause in his narrative. The reason for the noise was disclosed when a Mr Henry Hunt, a sympathizer with the aims of the National Union, entered the court room and sat down. The coroner paid no apparent attention and Thomas continued.

'I said to Mr Stallwood, "you are doing a great deal of harm, pray do not go on so." He said "Why did you not read the Riot Act?" I told him I was not present when the mischief occurred, nor was any of my division. Mr Stallwood still continued to indulge in his observations. The impression on my mind was that he had taken too much wine. My feelings were much excited at what I had seen and I said "It is through such fellows as you that so much mischief is produced".'

Superintendent Thomas then described how he took Stallwood to the Calthorpe Arms to see Culley's body, he was positive that Stallwood had declared that he was a magistrate.

The Clerkenwell Riot

Juror—'From whom did you receive orders to go to the ground?'

Thomas—'The orders I received were written orders. I received them through my clerk from the Commissioners.'

Juror—'By whom were the orders signed?'

Thomas—'The orders are generally signed with the initials of one or both of the Commissioners, and I presume they were so signed on this occasion.'

Juror—'During the time you were there, what refreshment did the men partake of?'

Thomas—'Some porter was brought, but I cannot say what quantity; it, however, fell short of half a pint each man. Some of the men had no money to pay for beer, and they went without.'

Juror—'Was any order given for them to have as much beer as they liked?'

Thomas—'Most decidedly not.'

Juror—'Do you mean to say that the men of the other divisions had only had a pint of beer each?'

Thomas—'I don't know what drink the men belonging to the other divisions had. I only attended to my own division. I know they had no more than half a pint each, as four joined together and had a pot between them.'

Juror—'Did you take your orders with you?'

Thomas—'They merely stated the amont of force that was to proceed to the riding school.'

Juror—'Then you had a discretionary power as to what you were to do?'

Thomas—'My orders were to assemble my men in the riding school and then wait for further orders.'

Juror—'Did you receive orders to take possession of the ground previous to the meeting?'

Thomas—'No.'

Juror—'Did you see any persons lying on the ground bleeding?'

Thomas—'One man came to me with his head bleeding when I was speaking to Mr Stallwood and he said "What am I to do with this?" I advised him to go to a doctor.'

Mary Hamilton was next sworn. She said that she was a ser-

The Fourth Day of the Inquest

vant at the Magpie and Stump, in Fetter Lane, and that she had gone to Cold Bath Fields to see the meeting.

'I came through the posts in Calthorpe Street and, on going up the right hand side, between three and four o'clock in the afternoon, I met the policeman who is now dead. While I was talking to him I perceived a man rush towards him from the mob with something in his hand, with which he made a thrust at the policeman, but I could not distinguish what it was. The man said "I shall do for the bugger". I said "For God's sake let me get out" and I hastened away as fast as I could. I saw the deceased after he was dead and knew him to be the same who spoke to me. The instrument which the man had who rushed towards me was like an instrument used to sharpen knives on. I was knocked down and my clothes were torn. The man who stabbed the policeman was a pale thin-visaged man with a long nose, and he seemed very ferocious. I did not take particular notice of the man who rushed towards the deceased and should not know him again. I do not know who knocked me down. I was not struck. The instrument appeared like a butcher's steel and was as long as my finger.'

Juror—'Then it may have been a piece of wire for ought you know?'

Coroner, roused,—'The witness has said nothing about wire. Good God, gentlemen, witnesses are not to be treated in this way.'

Mary Hamilton—'I did not see the policeman strike the man first, nor had he said anything to him to provoke him. I do not know how the man was dressed. I saw flags and banners but the man who stabbed the deceased did not carry any. I am positive that the thrust was made at the deceased's left side. I was taken by an inspector to see the place where the man was stabbed. I am sure that the policeman saw the man that made a rush upon him. He held up something in his hand but I cannot tell whether it was his staff or not.'

There seems to have been considerable doubt as to who was really organizing the witnesses at the inquest. This is normally the responsibility of the coroner, who should have seen statements and have some notion as to what the witnesses are going to

The Clerkenwell Riot

say so that he can exercise some selection. The haste with which this important case was handled once more appears evident from the coroner's next remark, uttered when the name of the next witness was called.

'Gentlemen, how many witnesses would you have? How many do you want? It has already been proved that the poor man was stabbed and murdered. It would have saved you two days' time if you had had that girl called before who last gave evidence.'

Mr Alexander, a juror—'I differ from you, Sir, I don't think it would.'

Coroner—'But I think it would.'

Alexander—'But I don't; and if I must speak my mind, I don't believe one iota of what she said.'

Coroner—'But I do. She has sworn it, and I am bound to believe her. At all events, there is one fact established which cannot be disputed, namely, that the poor man was stabbed in cold blood and with a dagger.'

James Yewett, of Great Wild Street, an Inspector to the Animal's Friend Society, said he was in the neighbourhood calling on a friend when he saw a great rush of people from Calthorpe Street, he saw police with staves and stood in the doorway of the Calthorpe Arms. Someone said that a policeman had been stabbed and he saw Culley drop down at the door. With two other people he helped him into the yard. Yewett saw the blood trickling from Culley and asked him if he was stabbed and he said he was.

Later in the afternoon on his way home a man in Great Queen Street, Lincoln's Inn Fields, told him he had seen the stabbing. He saw two police officers approaching and reported the matter to them, but they went on without paying any attention.

Coroner—'Did you ask the man his name and address?'
Yewett—'No.'
Coroner—'And why not?'
Yewett—'I thought that as they did not take notice of matter, that I would not trouble myself about it.'
Coroner—'But you ought to have done so. What sort of man was he?'

The Fourth Day of the Inquest

Yewett—'An elderly man, with a snuff-coloured coat. When he found I was a little inquisitive, he made away; and besides, if I had pressed him for his name, he would have given a false one. He had a pale face and a long nose.'

A juror—'I should have taken him into custody.'

The irrepressible Mr Nathaniel Stallwood here presented himself before the coroner and said that he had received a note by the twopenny post that morning from a person who acknowledged himself to be the murderer of Culley and who stated that his eye had been knocked out. Mr Stallwood felt it his bounden duty to lay the letter before the court.

The coroner read the letter himself, but refused to allow it to be read out publicly, saying it could not be legal evidence.

Foreman of the jury—'Mr Coroner, it is the wish of myself and brother jurors to adjourn until to-morrow.'

Coroner—'There can be no question of it, we shall continue the hearing.'

Mr Henry Hunt, the intruder, then spoke loudly about someone named Fricker who had some very important evidence to give. The sergeant-beadle, Keys, after repeatedly telling Hunt to be quiet said 'If you are not quiet, Sir, I shall turn you out of the room'. The coroner, with asperity, informed Hunt that his interference was improper.

Now the foreman of the jury said that the jury wished to know whence the orders on which the police acted originated.

Coroner—'Why, you have had that explained, as much as it can be, already. Superintendent Thomas has told you that the Commissioner's clerk makes out an order in writing, which is sent round to his superintendents, and they act upon it.'

Foreman—'Yes, but it would appear that the superintendents act upon those orders as they please, and according to their own notions.'

Alexander, a juror—'I think it very important to ascertain whether any Secretary of State is justified in causing 1700 policemen to be marched in amongst a peaceable crowd.'

The Clerkenwell Riot

Coroner—'There were not so many.'

Alexander—'Yes, Sir, it has been proved there were 1700.'

Coroner—'So much the better, if it was an unlawful assembly.'

Juror—'We wish to ascertain what Lord Melbourne's orders were to Colonel Rowan and Mr Mayne, and whether those orders were acted upon strictly as they were received; if they were not, we shall know where the blame lies.'

Another juror—'I, for my part, am determined not to give a verdict until that point is ascertained.'

Foreman, rising to his full height and pointing to a Mr Gude, who was sitting near the coroner—'Did not that gentleman say "Then we must have another jury?"'

Mr Gude—'I said no such thing.'

Foreman—'I put it to you as a man of honour, Sir, that you did not utter those words.'

Mr Gude—'I did not in allusion to this jury.'

Several jurors—'Oh! Oh! What jury then, could you have alluded to?'

Foreman—'Will you again say, Sir, that you did not utter the words I have mentioned?'

Mr Gude—'I have already said so.'

Foreman—'Then, Sir, I am bound to tell you that it is not true, for I heard you say the words, and will swear to them.'

A juror remarked that Mr Gude ought to leave the room.

Foreman—'I shall tell the gentleman this much; we are quite ready to disperse if the coroner thinks proper to discharge us, but no consideration will intimidate us from pursuing our proper course of duty. So long as we do remain here we shall act upon the dictates of our own consciences.'

Mr Gude's withdrawal from the room was not insisted on.

A succession of senior police officers next were questioned about their orders and whence they originated. There were a number of other witnesses brought in but, as it was obvious that they knew nothing about the circumstances of Culley's death, they were not examined.

Robert Fawcett, a constable of C division, who was near Superintendent Baker when the Superintendent was attacked by a man with a Maceroni pike, explained how he had knocked the assailant

The Fourth Day of the Inquest

down. He said 'I would have knocked my own father down under the same circumstances'.

Foreman—'We have not the least doubt of that. We are sure you would be quite capable of such an act.'

Mr Alexander, the vociferous juror—'There are a great many like you in the force, I am sorry to say.'

Fawcett—'I thought it was time to do so when I saw Mr Baker about to be stabbed.'

Coroner—'And I think so too.'

Fawcett—'I had no more than one pint of porter on that day.'

Two police officers stated that they had been struck by stones.

Juror—'How came there to be so many brickbats handy? Are the streets there paved?'

Coroner—'There are plenty in the waste ground and besides, you know, if you want to beat a dog it is easy to find a stick for him.'

Police Constable Samuel A'Court, of C division, gave evidence of how he met Culley on the right-hand side of Calthorpe Street and how Culley had said 'Tom, I am stabbed, I am done'; after this A'Court was attacked by two men, one of whom came from the same direction as Culley. This man struck at him with a weapon but he could not say what it was. The man was wearing a snuff-coloured coat and drab trousers.

One of the jury then asked for a five minutes' adjournment. The coroner refused this, saying that there were still plenty of witnesses waiting to be examined.

Alexander, the juror—'Yes, Sir, but we can hear them better when we have had some refreshment.'

A series of police officers now testified to seeing members of the mob armed with bludgeons and to seeing a variety of stones thrown. Most of the police officers had received heavy blows from clubs or stones.

Two further members of the public came forward and said that they had been beaten by groups of policemen and then a proclamation was made inviting witnesses to come forward and give evidence. No one answered this proclamation although it was said that a number of people had attended and applied to be heard.

Coroner—'Then it appears to me, gentlemen, that you have arrived at the end of your labours.'

XII

The End of the Inquest

The atrabiliousness which pervaded the hearing was, essentially, an expression of hatred and mistrust of the have-nots for the haves. The police, though drawn from the working classes, were disliked from both sides, for, as has been observed, they regulated anti-social behaviour of rich and poor alike. The opinions of Jeffery, the witness who spoke of the necessity for security, were not widely held in 1833.

Where did Stallwood fit in? He was an opportunist, devoted to profit, with social ambitions which had been frustrated by his own dishonesty and greed. He clearly included the police in his rancour against the established order of things. He had lost no time in passing the letter which he produced at the inquest to the Press. The text of the letter, which was anonymous, was published in *The Times* of May 21, 1833, the day after the jury reached their verdict in Culley's inquest.

May 19, 1833

'Dear Sir—You will not, I hope, take it as too great a liberty for an individual to address to you a few lines, that I may give you some account of the manner in which the policeman met with his death on last Monday, and how two other policemen were wounded. And that because I have heard from my surgeon that men have been charged with the act. I was there last Monday when the police came up and beat the people, and blocked up every passage and struck without distinction old and young, though every individual tried to make his escape from the ground. I myself tried, and was desperately beaten by policemen, and my head was dreadfully cut in half a dozen places, the bridge of my nose completely smashed and my left eye hanging out of the socket. I was forced to despair when I saw myself nearly surrounded by the police. In this distressing state I darted the blade which I had in my walking stick, and began to fight like a man in despair to save my life, and I at last found means to effect my escape. In this desperate state I killed the policeman and wounded two others. When I was some distance from the field of action my wife met me and cried out "Good Lord, John, what is the matter?" I then took my handkerchief and showed my eye to her and told her that the police had nearly dashed out my brains, when she immediately got me home and sent for the surgeon, who dressed my wounds for me, which he would not receive any pay, but has ever since attended on me and given food also to my wife and children in a very liberal manner, and swore never to disclose what I told him.

'My body is lying on a dying bed and has taken me one day to write this letter, being very ill and weak, and it causes me great pain to be lifted up in bed. I have not the use of my left arm, being so desperately beaten by the policemen that I cannot move it, and my left eye, though set, I believe that if I should survive I shall never be able to see with it again. My surgeon has told me not to sign my name, nor mention my place of abode, as the magistrates would proceed against me and hang me if they could. He has told me too that as long as I am unwell he will support my wife and family and pay my rent. I cannot, dear Sir, say more, begging that you make it known, because of men that may suffer for what I have done, and you may depend that what is here related is true. Adieu, dear Sir.

Addressed to Nathaniel Stallwood, Esq., Calthorpe Street.'

Although the coroner's jury had reached their verdict when this was printed it is surprising that this anonymous letter was published while proceedings against George Fursey were pending. It may be said straight away that the author of this sensational note was never traced but it added more fuel to the rumour and fabrication which surrounded the Cold Bath Fields affray.

When Mr Stirling, the coroner, began his summing up the court had sat without a break from just after ten o'clock in the morning until past six o'clock in the evening. The atmosphere was highly unfavourable to calm deliberation and tempers were frayed from deprivation of food and drink and from fatigue. The

The End of the Inquest

rumour that a verdict was soon to be expected had drawn a huge crowd to the streets surrounding the Calthorpe Arms and the murmurs of the multitude penetrated into the stifling court room.

The foreman of the jury said 'The only difficulty that appears to us in the matter at present is, that we think it desirable to ascertain the nature of the orders which were originally given by the Commissioners of police, for the prevention or suppression of the meeting.'

The Coroner dealt with this matter and swept on into his summing up.

'What has that to do with it, what the original orders were? You have it in evidence that papers were issued calling a meeting for a purpose in effecting which, no doubt, a great many would be glad to participate, but which the proclamation of the Secretary of State declared to be illegal; and you have seen those papers giving the people very good advice to stay away from the meeting, and it is a very unfortunate thing that so many people were so foolish as to go to that meeting after having received that advice because, indeed, it had not been given in the form which they considered perfect and legal. You have it also in evidence that the police were directed to attend there to prevent the meeting. That it was not a very innocent meeting was proved by the fact that the chairman thought it necessary to use the precaution of asking for a provision for his wife and family, and to advise the people not to break the peace.

'Afterwards they came with banners and flags, bearing inscriptions of 'Death or Liberty'. The police attempted to take those banners, resistance was made, the police were struck with stones, brickbats and bludgeons, which you have seen, and even daggers were used, a mode of assault which is foreign to this country. In that manner three men have been stabbed, and amongst them the unfortunate man respecting whose death you have been summoned to inquire. A woman has proved to you that she was standing in Calthorpe Street in conversation with the deceased, who was peaceably giving her the best advice, when a man separated from the crowd and, without any provocation, using at the same time a most coarse expression, stabbed the deceased with an instrument which she believes to be a steel, such as butchers use to sharpen their knives on. She was thrown down by the press of the mob and she saw no more of the deceased.

'Other witnesses have given you an account of the deceased to the moment when he died; and the nature of the wound has been so described to you to be such as the instrument spoken of would inflict. The immediate cause of the deceased's death was that this instrument had cut into a great vein and the man bled to death. If you can find any justification for this act, it is more than I can. The only witness who can pretend to have seen the blow struck is the young woman.

'Now, upon this evidence it is for you to say what caused the man's death. The person who inflicted the wound carried a weapon certainly not with any peaceable intention. If you are of opinion that the deceased met his death from that weapon in the way described I think you will feel it your duty to bring in a verdict of wilful murder, but that is for you to consider; and if you have been unable to ascertain by whose hand the blow was struck, you will bring in a verdict of wilful murder against some person or persons unknown.

'If any juror wishes the evidence to be read over, of course I shall read it, but you have all paid so much attention to the evidence that I hardly think such a course is now necessary. The case itself lies in a nutshell. You will, of course, wish to consult together and, if you desire it, I shall order this room to be cleared; but if you prefer to retire to another room, there is one adjoining which I will order to be prepared for you.'

The jury elected to withdraw and left the court room at six minutes to seven in the evening. In half an hour the jury sent a message that sixteen of the seventeen members were agreed on a verdict condemnatory of the police. An hour later a second message said that there was no prospect of their agreement. The coroner said that they would agree when they became a little more hungry; the jury repeated their communication several times, but with no change in the coroner's attitude.

The coroner's summing up was unexceptionable. The jury's sole function was to find the legal nature of Culley's death and the facts were clear enough; the wound could not have been self-inflicted and it was obviously meant to injure severely if not to kill. The only possible verdict on the evidence was murder by a person or persons unknown. However, the jury had set out to make the affair into a political issue and to condemn the police

The End of the Inquest

as roundly as they could. Although the coroner's interpretation of the law was correct, throughout the hearing he failed to exert his authority over the court. Not much can be found about Mr Stirling but he is said to have had the reputation of being a good lawyer and an experienced coroner, but he was advanced in years. The situation demanded a firm hand, and the least he might have done was to have adjourned his inquest and held it in a less emotionally charged place.

The seemingly callous remark, that the jury would reach an agreement when they became more hungry was, likewise, accepted practice at the time. The first edition of Jervis on Coroners, published in 1829, states laconically 'But it may so happen that the twelve cannot agree, in which case the jury are to be kept without meat, drink or fire until they return their verdict. Even this may sometimes be ineffectual.' We treat our juries more indulgently nowadays.

At half past nine the jury came in with a paper on which they had caused their verdict to be written in the following terms:—

'We find a verdict of *justifiable homicide* on these grounds—that no Riot Act was read, nor any proclamation advising the people to disperse; that the Government did not take the proper precautions to prevent the meeting from assembling; and that the conduct of the police was ferocious, brutal and unprovoked by the people; and we moreover, express our anxious hope that the Government will, in future, take better precautions to prevent the recurrence of such disgraceful transactions in the Metropolis.'

The court room rocked with cheering, the crowds in the street took up the sound until it seemed that the whole neighbourhood was echoing with excitement. It was some time, despite strenuous efforts by the beadle and the police present, before any semblance of order could be restored. It was a preposterous verdict, quite unjustifiable, and the comments about the Government and the behaviour of the police were right outside the jury's powers. They realized that popular opinion was with them, and took full advantage of the backing of which they felt assured. For the moment, the Rule of Law was set at naught. The coroner said—'I do not know how you can say all these things on the evidence you have heard. The only evidence which you have had to show you how this man met his death was that young woman, who saw the stab given to a man who was acting in a laudable and unoffending manner; and how any one on that jury can justify such an act I do not understand. I hope, gentlemen, you will reconsider your verdict. You are not here to try the conduct of other persons, whether in the Government or the police. This, in my opinion, is no verdict.'

There was a renewed outburst of insolent laughter and jeers of 'Oh! Oh! Isn't it? Oh! Oh! Indeed!'

The Coroner—'It was not justifiable homicide; it was rather wilful murder by some one you do know or someone you don't know.'

More disturbance and shouting, which was only quelled with great difficulty.

Foreman—'We have patiently considered our verdict; there have been conflicting opinions among us, but we have all anxiously compared our opinions and that is the conscientious verdict of us all, patiently and carefully formed with the most anxious deliberation.'

Coroner—'You are called upon to say how Robert Culley came to his death, and the only evidence you have to decide upon that is that of the young woman who saw him stabbed. Several of the jury exclaimed—'We do not believe her—no, not one of us!'

Coroner—'And why not?'

Juror—'Because she was contradicted by other witnesses. She said she was two minutes talking to the policeman and it was proved that that was impossible by all the other witnesses. She was tutored.'

Another juror—'She was tutored by the police, she acknowledged having been with them ever since that day. Why ask us to give a verdict against our consciences?'

Foreman—'We are all of opinion that if a hundred policemen had occupied the ground this man would not have been slain.'

A juror—'We only wonder that there were not more lives lost.'

Coroner—'Well, gentlemen, your verdict is "that Robert Culley was killed with justifiable homicide"?'

Jurors—'Aye, that it is.'

Coroner—'Well, I shall strike out all the rest.' And he was seen

The End of the Inquest

to draw his pencil through all the words that followed 'justifiable homicide'.

Foreman—'I cannot agree to that, Sir.'

Jurors—'Nor any of us.'

Foreman—'Before God and our country, on our solemn oaths, we have given the subject all the consideration in our power; and the paper which I have handed to you contains the judgment in which we are unanimously agreed. If you strike out any part of that it is not our verdict.'

Coroner—'So you say it was justifiable homicide because some persons broke other persons' heads some half an hour after the man was murdered?'

A juror—'We are not of opinion that the heads were not broken until after the man was killed. If you record any verdict without the whole of what we say, it will not be a true verdict.'

Another juror—'What occasion was there to swear us, and keep us away all these days from our business and families if it is to be the coroner's verdict, and not the jury's?'

Several of the jury—'You had better dismiss us if you won't take our verdict.'

Foreman—'And the sooner the better. We are fatigued to exhaustion; we have done our duty laboriously and faithfully, and our country can expect no more of us.'

Coroner—'Well! So—you did your duty by giving in a verdict to say that a man is justified in stabbing an unoffending man.'

Foreman—'If proper measures had been taken, either by reading the Riot Act, or a proclamation, or any other means, we would not bring in a verdict to justify the homicide. Therefore, to let that verdict go abroad alone would be very dangerous, and it might be thought that we justified the stabbing a policeman who was legally employed.'

Coroner—'I think that is the fact.'

Foreman—'No, on the contrary, we wish to give the police every protection.'

Coroner—'Do you call these remarks a recommendation? Why, you are finding fault with everybody with a vengeance. What reason was there to stab the man?'

Juror—'Mr Coroner, do you not recollect that before there was any stabbing or throwing of stones, or any other violence, a man rushed out from the body of police and violently struck about him, having said to those behind him "Now, go it, boys!"? We are of opinion from the evidence that this was the same man.'

Certainly as no such thing had been given in evidence, it seems that the jury was taking note of local gossip. The court room lapsed into a moody silence, the coroner busied himself with his papers. The jury studied the backs of their hands and shuffled their feet. No one looked anyone else in the face and the atmosphere was as disagreeable as could be. Eventually a juror said 'Mr Coroner, we have become as quiet as a Quaker's meeting. May we go, or have you any other little job for us?' there was an outburst of laughter. The coroner said 'You may go when you agree to your verdict.'

Foreman—'Mr Coroner, we have as strong an impression of the importance of our duty as any men can have, and we have agreed to our verdict and will agree to none other.'

Coroner—'So you think that a meeting to overturn the Government was a justification of the homicide?'

Foreman—'No, Sir, far from it. We are all of us men who have families and some stake in the country. Indeed, I think there is none of us but have some little property. We all of us are of one opinion about the impropriety of that meeting and we are far from liking mob meetings. If the police had acted with propriety we would all of us have turned out to assist and protect them at any risk.'

Coroner—'There were proclamations forbidding the meeting posted all over the town.'

A juror—'I am on my oath, Sir, and I say that I saw some of those posted on the Tuesday, the day after the meeting.' This sally produced a further laugh.

Coroner—'Instead of inquiring how the man was killed you are trying the police and other people for quite different things.'

Foreman—'It is the conduct of those people which justifies us in giving that verdict. If precautions had been taken properly, there would have been no murder.' This after the jury were insisting that this was no murder but a justifiable homicide.

Coroner—'How do you think you can justify a man for murdering this policeman, who offended no one and who was giving advice to that woman whom we heard?'

The End of the Inquest

Several jurors all speaking at once—'Her evidence was disproved. She is not worthy of credit.'

A single juror—'I have seen her drinking gin on the leads of this house with a crowd of policemen, with whom she admits she has been since the day of the meeting.'

Another juror—'She is still there drinking, though she swore this morning that she was in a hurry to go home as she had been ordered not to stay too long.'

Foreman—'We can give no other verdict. We are of opinion that this man would not have lost his life had proper measures been taken. No one saw the stab given; we are of opinion that it was given in the confusion which the violence of the man himself produced.'

Coroner—'But you can give a conscientious verdict without libelling anyone.'

Foreman—'It is no libel.'

Coroner—'It certainly appears that there was a good deal of knocking about on one side and the other.'

Foreman—'It was all on one side.'

Coroner—'Why! The police did not stab.'

Foreman—'Mr Coroner, we are unanimously of opinion that if they had acted with moderation the deceased would not have been stabbed. The woman who swears otherwise we do not believe. It is plain she was tutored and the little girl who was brought up to tell us she saw the stab given, young and ignorant as she was, was still artful enough to keep back the important fact that the man who stabbed the policeman was violently assaulted first.'

There was another long silence. Many persons left the room and a loud voice was heard outside explaining to the crowd the state of affairs in the Court room and the terms of the verdict. There was a deafening outburst of cheering which brought the proceedings absolutely to a standstill. When the noise had abated somewhat the foreman of the jury resumed. 'In the name of my brother jurors, I have to repeat that we have considered our verdict and it is the only one in which, upon the evidence, we should feel ourselves justified. Let me refer you, Sir, to the evidence of Mr Goore. You will recollect, Sir, the treatment he received and the remarkable expression he used, that if he had a weapon he would have felt himself justified in using it and when he saw how the fellows behaved he said he would have cut their heads off.'

The Coroner remained silent, the jury became more restive and muttered to each other. One juror said 'So help me, God, I am ready to faint—I have fasted since ten o'clock this morning. I have had nothing but a glass of water. It is a shame to treat us this way. If you will not have our verdict dismiss us, for if you keep me here for a year I cannot, with respect to my oath, alter that verdict.'

Coroner—"Reconsider your verdict.'

Juror—'You have kept us here an hour and a half to no purpose. If you think we are unfit to give a sound verdict call a more able jury.'

Coroner—'Surely you could give a justifying verdict and say that you did so for reasons peculiar to this case; but it is not right to give this verdict which is slandering people you have no right to try.'

Juror—'Our reasons we have given, they are on that paper. If we say that it is justifiable homicide without that rider it would appear that we approved of any brutal fellow stabbing a policeman in the ordinary execution of his duty and that we would encourage illegal meetings. We will not consent to any such verdict.'

Coroner—'You throw all the blame on the police, but what do you say of the people who stabbed them? This verdict goes to excite the people against the police. You call them brutal and ferocious and every epithet to make them odious.'

Foreman—'It has been proved in evidence that their conduct was such.'

Coroner—'I think the first part goes a great way without the rest when you say that this homicide was justifiable.'

Juror—'I see no use in a jury if one man can set aside their verdict.'

Coroner—'Your verdict only traduces the police and the Government. You are not born out by the evidence in justifying the murder of this man. Were the people innocent who used the murderous weapons, stilettos, bludgeons and lances, such as you have seen?'

Foreman—'We state in our verdict on what grounds we justify

The End of the Inquest

the homicide. We do not traduce the police nor the Government. We trust that our verdict will prevent the negligence and misconduct which has caused the arms and heads of His Majesty's peaceable subjects to be broken.'

Coroner—'Do you call them peaceable subjects?'

Foreman—'It has been proved that they were peaceable. We will say no more, Sir, record our verdict or dismiss us. We have told you, Sir, we will not alter a letter. Let us pass no more time in this trifling contention as we have passed nearly two hours. We have fasted since ten o'clock this morning and we protest against this treatment. If you will not have our verdict please yourself, as you have the power. Dismiss us and produce an abler jury and let God and our country decide between us!' Loud and prolonged cheering, which was taken up by the throngs outside in the streets.

The Coroner now carried on an earnest conversation in undertones with his clerk and the foreman of the jury. The verdict as originally put in was recorded and the inquisition and depositions signed.

Coroner—'Gentlemen, I consider your verdict disgraceful to you but I thank you for your great attention to this case.' The foreman, who was not to be outdone in courtesy, bowed to the Coroner and replied 'We thank you, Sir.'

Immediately those present in the room called out 'Bravo, jurors, you have done your duty nobly, the country is indebted to you' and the shouts and cheering were renewed. The jurors filed down the narrow stairs and, as they passed through the bars, pots of ale were pressed upon them and many of the bystanders surged forward to shake each man by the hand. It was now after eleven o'clock, they had been in the Calthorpe Arms for more than twelve hours without a break. Small impromptu torchlight processions were formed to escort each juror back to his home and the excitement in the streets was intense. All thought that a tremendous victory for liberty had been won. The only thing that was defeated for the time being was the rule of law: and a policeman was dead, leaving behind a young pregnant widow. As the police left the inn they were hooted.

XIII

After the Verdict

Although the members of the jury could not have made themselves clearer, their verdict of justifiable homicide was not only perverse but also inappropriate. Killing is only justifiable when the situation is such that public justice cannot be advanced without it, as sometimes occurs in the arrest of a dangerous criminal, control of a riot or in judicial execution. Where death is incidental to reasonable self-defence the homicide is said to be excusable. In earlier times the law showed lenience to a man who resisted arrest if there was a doubt about the strict legality of a law officer's action; in their zeal to protect the rights of the citizen, the courts would not be slow to regard such resistance—even if the law officer was killed—as self-defence against a potentially deadly onslaught.

While it is improbable that this legal attitude was known to the crowds which assembled at Cold Bath Fields, this approval of independence of authority was characteristic of the age and inimical to the police.

A killing is excusable on the grounds of self-defence if the person attacked retreats until he backs into a wall and he can go no further, and if the amount of force he uses is no more than is absolutely necessary. Colonel Rowan had taken good care that those attending the meeting had ample opportunity for escape and he had instructed his men to use a minimum of force. Mary Hamilton was the only person who swore to seeing the assailant stab Culley, if Mary Ann Perkins is excluded. Her description was clearly one of unprovoked assault and, for what it was worth, there was no question of the attacker having to defend himself

After the Verdict

against Culley. However, the jury, who heard her and observed her demeanour, came to the reasonable conclusion that her evidence was fabricated. Setting aside Mary Hamilton's evidence, it still could not be maintained that the infliction of a lethal stab wound on a man armed only with a stave, was reasonable self-defence, especially as avenues of escape had been deliberately left open.

The next morning, Tuesday, May 21, 1833 *The Times* printed some notices to correspondents:—

'B, who sends a letter about the policeman Culley, should have gone before the Coroner's jury.'

'The letter signed "A vestryman of St Pancras" is, we have no doubt, true, but it would subject us to an action.' Did this contain more revelations about Mr Stallwood?

' "A member", who writes a personal letter, should give his name.'

The Times leader writer was unable to see any reason for the verdict of justifiable homicide and commented that

'The conversation which passed after the verdict, exhibits the jury in the character of men who were influenced by a strong though, we think, mistaken sense of duty, while their observations on the Riot Act demonstrate their ignorance of the law relating to illegal assemblies.'

Referring to comments in the French Press about the affray *The Times*, in gay and sarcastic mood, warned the French Republicans that the British were not on the highway to join them in democratic polity. The hopes of those who dreamed of barricades and paving stones, aroused by the treasonable designs of the two monosyllables Mee and Lee on a lamppost, were doomed to disappointment. No dictator or president had yet been hatched to change the Government or to guide the new republic, and the staves of the police dispersed the whole embryo army in three minutes.

The Mr Russell who called the meeting gave no indication as to the form the proposed convention was to take. *The Times* felt

The Clerkenwell Riot

ashamed to dignify such wretched absurdities with the name of treason, although strictly the proposition was treasonable because the Utopian patriot proposed to dispense with the existing Parliament and the existing monarchy. To those simple working men who assembled at Cold Bath Fields the National Convention appeared only a meeting to petition against existing taxes. But had the Mees and Lees acting under the phantom patriot Russell been allowed to collect a mob and pass resolutions, the account of their proceedings (magnified by rumour) might have produced an effect at home and on the continent; credulous and timid men could well have believed England to be on the brink of revolution. It was as right, therefore, to disperse this illegal mob before they had adopted any of their absurd resolutions, as it was wrong to disperse it with unnecessary violence. Had they been allowed to decree a National Convention the few hundreds present would have been magnified into 20,000 freemen.

Common sense, ultimately, has always been a cardinal British characteristic even though it sometimes goes to sleep for long periods. *The Times* did a great national service in quickly lowering the temperature raised by the intransigent stand of the jury at the inquest on Robert Culley. The identity of John Russell, who purported to sign the notice of the public meeting at Cold Bath Fields, was never discovered. There is a distinct possibility that he was a fictitious personality. Certainly the printing was done by the young man Lee, for his name appears at the bottom left hand corner of the notice; and the quality of the layout and type is inferior to that of the Government notice, as might be expected from work done on a press kept in his own home. It was still not at all clear as to what the meeting was to have been about.

The next day, Wednesday, May 22, 1833, *The Times* leader was painfully serious. It quoted the inquest jury's rider that no Riot Act was read, that there was no proclamation advising the people to disperse, that the Government made no attempt to prevent the meeting from assembling and that the police behaved brutally. Had these allegations been true, Culley's murderer (and the word was used openly despite the verdict) was armed with a lethal weapon before he knew there would be no Riot Act; before he knew there would be no proclamation, before he knew the meeting would be dispersed and before he knew the police would act ferociously. Had he struck Culley with his fist and killed him

After the Verdict

unintentionally there would be something to be said for the jury's attitude but it was clear that the killer went armed with the intention of shedding blood. If this verdict were lawful it would give licence to members of the public to attend all meetings armed. *The Times* entreated members of the jury to search their consciences, for some of them had acted as jurymen, witnesses, coroners and bystanders all at once, crying out 'Shame!' incessantly.

It appeared that there was nothing in the evidence at the inquest on which a verdict of justifiable homicide could be founded. *The Times* agreed with the jury in regarding Mary Hamilton's evidence as unworthy of credit. The meeting was unlawful and nothing could sanction the use of deadly weapons in repelling an onslaught by police.

'To say the truth, we have been led by recent information to believe that unnecessary violence was resorted to on the part of the police. They were provoked too soon—they were probably alarmed beyond what right reason, or a knowledge of the real insignificance of the meeting, would dictate; and like other potentates under the influence of terror, indemnified themselves with cruelty for the pain of fright, and broke all the heads about them as a protection to their own. This is sufficiently melancholy, but why was it not prevented?'

The leading article went on to speculate on the failure of Colonel Rowan to restrain police violence—could there not have been a mild and manly expostulation with the crowd? The very magnitude of the police force present should have led to its being deployed with moderation and forbearance. The mismanagement was so great that public sympathy went with those who had acknowledgedly violated the law, and adversely to those whose business was to enforce it. The verdict might be salutary of a lesson of temper to the police but it would not increase the confidence of discriminating minds in the sagacity of juries.

'Indeed, when we consider the not improbable consequence of the verdict in encouraging low ruffians to resist authority, we think that the jury, who represent themselves as having some stake in the country, may before long lament that their anxiety to repress the violence of power has made them disregard the law of the land—the surest protector of the poor against the rich no less than of the rich against the poor.'

It is always easy to be wise after an event. *The Times'* criticism of the police was unworthy. It was wrong to suggest that the police thought the meeting insignificant. On the contrary, the Commissioners knew that it would be attended by many known bad characters and supporters of subversive movements. In the prevailing political climate the threat of a national convention was ominous and the Commissioners had been instructed by the Home Secretary to apprehend the ringleaders.

It was ridiculous to impute terror to the police. Colonel Rowan, a professional soldier of experience, made his plans carefully and moved out the police columns with precision when he had judged the right moment. Was it likely that veterans of Waterloo in considerable strength would quail at the spectacle of an unorganized mob? Colonel Rowan was resolved that the police should not fail and he may have mustered more men than was necessary, but he could not have forecast the size of the illegal meeting. It is noteworthy that, despite the wide publicity which the affray received, no member of the public complained of serious injury, if we except the fractured arm of Todd, and Wheeler, who received a scalp wound and produced clothing soaked in blood at the inquest. On the other hand one police officer was killed, two seriously wounded and a number received blows from bludgeons and stones.

On May 20th, Colonel Rowan submitted a somewhat apologetic report to the Home Office. In dealing with the reasons for *not* preventing people going to Cold Bath Fields he made several points. He stated that it would be difficult to distinguish between active Unionists and ordinary members of the public. If police had tried to stop everyone going to the Fields there might have been collisions with members of the public who happened to be passing that way legitimately; it was not desirable to interrupt a public thoroughfare. If the Unions were prevented from assembling at Cold Bath Fields and were really determined they would go elsewhere. The police would then have the choice of remaining and being useless or of accompanying the Unions and attracting large idle crowds *en route*.

After the Verdict

Colonel Rowan used strong language in describing members of the Unions. He said most of them were men of desperate character, without any regard or respect towards existing institutions or property. At their meetings language of the most inflammatory sort was used, and opportunities created for them to exercise their anti-social feelings. Hatred of the police was excited in all ways, all were advised and encouraged to arm themselves and to resist the police. It was well known to police that on this occasion many of the members of the unions would be armed.

Colonel Rowan went to Cold Bath Fields prepared to act, if necessary, in his capacity as magistrate. He had a copy of the Riot Act in his pocket and was ready to read out the prescribed proclamation. At two o'clock he estimated that 500 or 600 people were assembled and he was told that the Committee of the Unions was holding a meeting in the Union Tavern. He had various 'persons' sent to a distance to report if any of the classes were coming and was informed of the approach of groups from Lambeth and Whitechapel. He had police concealed in stable yards to avoid onlookers gathering. As one of the Union parties passed Busbridge's stables a stone was thrown, striking an inspector; a man was taken into custody.

Mee was identified to the Commissioner as a well-known leader among the Unions. When he addressed the meeting Colonel Rowan decided to break it up. He sent the first group of seventy men of A division into Calthorpe Street. When this group had gathered round the banners and the chairman of the meeting, he sent in the second detachment of 100 men, who were assailed by stones. The Commissioner then gave orders that Calthorpe Street was to be cleared. About this time he learned that three policemen had been stabbed.

The whole affair lasted about ten minutes but after this small parties of police moved about and, from time to time, took people into custody for throwing stones.

Much of the Commissioners' intelligence came from informers. For example, on May 21, 1833 they learned that a man named Mason, in Lambeth Walk opposite to the Cock and Bottle, manufactured spring daggers, knives and spearheads for the National Unions. However, it was not possible to take any legal action. There were also police spies. One of these, Popay, a former Lowestoft schoolteacher, was highly competent and attended a

The Clerkenwell Riot

number of meetings of classes of the National Union of the Working Classes without being detected. Popay marched with one of the processions to Cold Bath Fields and mingled with the crowd. These activities became known and attracted Parliamentary attention. Later in 1833 a Select Committee of the House of Commons condemned the practice of employing police spies.

Meanwhile the verdict of the jury was a lively topic in legal and government circles. A legal journal described it as 'monstrous affront to the principles of justice' and called for action. It was a simple matter to quash an inquest verdict for procedural error or refusal to receive relevant evidence. It was very different to upset a jury's verdict just because it was not generally acceptable. It was necessary for some person to apply to the Solicitor-General to issue his fiat for petition to the High Court to set aside the verdict, and good cause had to be shown. In Robert Culley's case who was to make the application? Would the coroner do it? Or could it be made on behalf of Culley's relatives? After consultation at high judicial level it was decided that King William IV himself was the most relevant person, since the issue was the King's peace. On May 30, 1833 the Solicitor-General petitioned the Court of King's Bench to quash the inquisition. The Court said without hesitation that the only verdict which could have been reached on the evidence was wilful murder by a person or persons unknown but never stated the grounds for quashing. The jury's verdict of justifiable homicide was set aside.

When a coroner's inquisition has been quashed the High Court normally directs the holding of a second inquest, either before the same coroner or another in the county. In Culley's case the Court contented itself with quashing and making some observations about murder. No second inquest was directed, with the result that to this day there is no verdict as to the legal nature of Culley's death.

The jury was still unwilling to let things alone. Greatly incensed, they petitioned Parliament on June 7th saying 'that they heard with great pain and alarm that their conscientious verdict had been quashed in the King's Bench and that a slur had been thereby cast on their character as jurymen acting under the solemn obligations of an oath and that they prayed the House to take the subject into consideration and pursue such means as

After the Verdict

might seem requisite to free the petitioners from blame and secure to future jurymen the privileges conferred on them by law.'

The result of this was the setting up of a select Committee of the House of Commons to inquire into the Cold Bath Fields affray; its deliberations will be considered later.

XIV

Another Political Meeting

On Friday, June 1, 1833, eighteen days after the affray, another political meeting was held at the Crown and Anchor Tavern in the Strand. This was arranged by the National Political Union for the purpose of considering the conduct of the Government and the police at Cold Bath Fields. The Crown and Anchor meeting was organized by Anti-Whigs who seized this golden opportunity to assail the Government with the ammunition provided by the affray. It was managed by skilled politicians of experience and education, who were resolved to exploit the situation to the full. By contrast, Cold Bath Fields was a crude affair, with indifferent speakers, attended by ruffians and uneducated crowds. Above all, this meeting was held indoors on enclosed premises. Apart from an Inspector Mallalieu, who attended in plain clothes, no police were present.

The company met in the evening in a large upstairs assembly room which was packed to capacity, it was estimated that 700 people were present. The proceedings were noisy and spirited but never got out of control and the chairman succeeded in keeping speakers more or less to the point. While the audience was waiting for the platform to be occupied there was much laughter and ribaldry. A man in the uniform of the Grenadier Guards attracted much attention. He went through the room selling copies of pamphlets *The Reformer* and the *Poor Man's Guardian* in which some inflammatory articles by Mee had been printed. The grenadier said he favoured reform: if the people rose up against the Government they had little to fear from his regiment, which was in sympathy with the working classes. The grenadier said he had been drummed out of his company for his political opinions

Another Political Meeting

after being confined for fourteen days in a damp dungeon with his hands and feet tied with ropes.

The platform was occupied by a number of members of Parliament and others known for extreme radical views. Mr John Arthur Roebuck was called upon to take the chair. Roebuck was at the time thirty-one years of age and had been called to the Bar two years before. In 1832 he was elected Radical Reform member for Bath. His subsequent political career was distinguished, he represented Sheffield for many years until his death in 1879. Although his vigorous methods in defending what he considered to be right earned him the nickname 'Tear 'em' he was, politically, developed far beyond the primitive mob orator and already showed the qualities of a skilful Parliamentarian. He was most violently opposed to the Whig Government.

Roebuck said that they were there, as private citizens, to consider what should be done about a violent infringement of one of their dearest privileges, by persons in authority. (Stamping and cries of 'hear, hear').

'Are we, my dear friends, to be deprived of our great constitutional privilege—that of assembling to debate topics of importance to our general welfare?' (Cheers) 'We must express our opinions on this latest great and violent infringement which was made at the meeting at Cold Bath Fields.' (Cheers) 'What, I ask you, would a good and paternal Government have done in the event of such a meeting taking place? In considering this you must have in view the state of the public mind at the period of that meeting. The meeting was called for the purpose of forming a National Convention. I am not going to consider whether that meeting was illegal or not—I freely tell you, my friends, that in my opinion it was strictly legal'! (Loud and prolonged cheers).

Mr Roebuck went on to say that the legality of the Cold Bath Fields meeting was not their concern at that moment but rather what a kindly and paternal Government would have done when such a meeting was to take place. Roebuck thought that the first persons with whom he would find fault were those who had called the meeting. Was their object likely to be achieved, or were they merely bringing their supporters into danger? He, Roebuck, would never have consented to bring the people into danger

The Clerkenwell Riot

where there was, as in that case, no chance of success. He, therefore, thought those who called the Cold Bath Fields meeting had been injudicious and that that was the sum and substance of their offence.

'What, then, ought the conduct of the Government to have been? The Government must, indeed, be mad—God knows, the present Government is foolish enough' (Cheers and laughter) 'If they thought there was any danger likely to arise from such a meeting. What had their paternal Government done? It had sent 1700 men to the meeting to disperse it; it had armed those men with weapons capable of inflicting painful and grievous wounds; it stimulated the men with drink and then these 1700 men attacked the unoffending people and beat them to the dust!' (Loud cheers).

Roebuck pointed out that the very same Government consisted of those who had thanked people, when its members were out of power, for holding meetings to put an end to the old unreformed Parliament. They were the last men who should have found fault with such meetings as Cold Bath Fields. Roebuck then explained the difference between an illegal and a legal meeting. He said that meetings to resist assessed taxes, for example, were illegal, for they resisted the law of the land. At the Cold Bath Fields meeting there was nothing contemplated which was against the law.

'Friends, I apprehend what is meant by a National Convention in France, or in America, but I have yet to learn that it is illegal in England. Why, what is a National Convention? I truly believe there is a National Convention at this very moment sitting here in London, in this town. It is called the Anti-Slavery Society, which is a convention from all parts of the Kingdom and whose object is to procure the emancipation of the slaves. I ask who is to decide whether the meeting was illegal or not? A parcel of ignorant men dressed in blue?' (Shouts and jeers) 'Not a great law officer, not men high in office whose opinions might be deserving of respect. No one asked the people quietly to disperse. No! All that was done was—' and here Mr Roebuck assumed a military demeanour 'Right about face, charge!' (Loud cheers and

Another Political Meeting

catcalls). 'I therefore consider myself justified in saying that the conduct of the police on that day was an illegal interference with the people when met to discuss their private affairs.'

Like most of those concerned with the Cold Bath Fields affair Roebuck was not meticulously accurate in his facts, neither was he very sensitive to the law of defamation, as his remarks about the coroner show.

'I shall not to-day say what I think about the conduct of the coroner who sat on the inquest held on the body of the policeman; in a few days I shall be in another place where I can give vent to my opinions with impunity and, depend on it, I shall do so. I will not say that the conduct of the coroner was overbearing' (hear, hear) 'or that he was ignorant or totally unfit for his situation, or partial; though you may, my friends, think all of that, because I may be prosecuted for saying so. I shall have another opportunity for stating my real opinions without fear.'

'The conduct of the jury in standing up for their unbiased opinion and the dignified manner in which they kept to that opinion without a single expression of passion, but merely saying that the verdict was their conscientious opinion and they could not, therefore, change it, reflected the greatest credit on them. I am proud to see a display of such sterling worth. I am convinced that, in interfering with that verdict, a greater blow has been struck at this existing Government than all the members of Parliament could inflict' (hear, hear) 'as it interfered with the expressed feelings of a great portion of the people.' (Loud and prolonged cheers as Mr Roebuck sat down wiping his brow).

Shouts from the back of the room caused heads to turn. A somewhat dishevelled person was seen waving his arms and calling out 'To hell with Parliament and to hell with the National Political Union!' After he was hustled out stumbling footsteps were heard on the stairs. He soon reappeared and received rougher treatment, his clothes were torn and he was kicked and hit, and finally thrown downstairs. It was later understood that this was no political partisan but merely a roisterer, elevated by too much drink, who had provided a diversion amusing to all but himself.

The Clerkenwell Riot

The next speaker was Daniel O'Connell, the Liberator, one of Ireland's most loyal patriots. O'Connell was born in 1775 and had years of experience behind him. He was called to the Irish Bar in 1798. Although his practice was enormous he still found time for conviviality and political agitation. A staunch catholic, his attacks on the Dublin Corporation resulted in a duel in which he killed his challenger. His remorse was lifelong and, though his fiery tongue brought him many another challenge, he refused all but one—from Peel in 1815. O'Connell's wife contrived his arrest and he was bound over to keep the peace, so no duel materialized. O'Connell organized the Catholic Association, which raised enough money to withstand the landowners on many occasions. He became Member for County Clare in 1828 but was unable to take his seat until 1830, as catholics were not admitted to Parliament until 1829. Although a liberal, he supported the Whigs in their reform policy. His interest in the matters which arose from the Cold Bath Fields affray is clear from his speech.

'I have come here tonight to discharge a duty which I don't know whether or not I owe to the people of England. I have come to rally public sentiment for the protection of your old and wise institution—trial by jury. Will you allow these Whigs to put down what your ancestors have fought for and which has been the protection of your rights and privileges for ages?' (Cheers). 'If you allow that you deserve to be slaves and, as you are now about to emancipate the slaves in the West Indies, I say that if you allow trial by jury to be put down you ought to have your faces blackened.' (Laughter)

Mr O'Connell said that trial by jury had been suppressed in Ireland by the Whigs, and for that he would never forgive them. Ireland, however, was neither frightened nor put down. The Whigs, the so-called defenders of liberty had suppressed trial by jury in Ireland. All that the present Government wishes to do was to establish a Whig despotism in the place of a Tory one. If the people wished to avoid this now was the time to make a stand.

'I said last week that the verdict of the jury at the inquest, and I stake upon this a reputation of thirty-five years at the Bar, was

Another Political Meeting

the only one which they could have given on the evidence as reported. The only verdict could be one of justifiable homicide and I repeat this to-day. If my reasons are not well founded I will allow you to scorn and despise me, I don't care what is said in the *Globe* or the *Morning Chronicle* (cries of '*The Times,* what about *The Times*?') Oh! Ha, Ha, *The Times,* it is past speaking of!' (hear, hear, hear) 'From the reported evidence I find that a meeting was called by people of whom I have never heard to establish (Heaven bless the mark!) a National Convention. There were seven and twenty obscure persons who called that meeting to establish a National Convention. It is a thing to be laughed at. A number of persons came to look on and laugh at the whole business, and women and children came likewise. There was another foolish thing called a proclamation, signed by no one. Good people, that thing brought more people together than the National Convention itself. There was not one single act of violence committed, nor one illegal word uttered. Before almost a word was said a number of men, calling themselves constables, made a sudden attack on men, women and children.' (Cheers).

'An affray took place, blood was streaming, and all that was known of the policeman's death was that a man was seen going back—back, good people, till he could go back no further, and all the time defending himself from the attack of the police; and that man, when he saw that there was no other way of avoiding death himself, did inflict death.' (Cheers). 'As a lawyer I would say that when the man had no other way of saving his own life but by the death of the aggressor, they could not bring in any other verdict. If the jury believed that the man killed the policeman only in self-defence, they would be perjured if they had given a different verdict.'

'What did the Whig Government do? They threw perjury into the teeth of the jury. They declared that which seventeen conscientious men declared on their oaths perjury. Those same persons who put down trial by jury in Ireland now have put down the verdict of that jury and declared them perjured.' (Cheers). 'I will give you one piece of advice. When you have meetings in future, have them within four walls, let them not be held out of doors, where spies and informers may come among you. If the persons who held the meeting for the formation of a National Convention had consulted me, O'Connell, I would have said

"Leave off your tomfoolery!". But I still doubt if it was illegal. Not a single lawyer in the Kingdom will deny what I have said.'

O'Connell was another who was not afraid to stretch the truth for his own purposes. He was a very able lawyer and, on the evidence, he must have realized he was stating the law incorrectly in the context of the Cold Bath Fields affray. His next remarks about His Majesty's judges would certainly have called for a rebuke from his Benchers had he been a member of the English Bar, but there is something rather splendid about the vigour of his language and, indeed of all those people who interested themselves in the reform movement.

'You must not be surprised at the conduct of the Court of King's Bench, if you look back into history where will you find a bench of judges not ready to side against the people (Loud and prolonged cheers). They always side with power, do these venerated judges. The judges quashed this inquest and I will tell you, good people, that this was the first instance in which such a proceeding has taken place without some persons coming forward and applying for it. I do not say the proceeding was wrong—it was the first on record. Was evidence put before the court?' (Loud shouts of "No! Never!") 'I shall blame all of you greatly if you do not get the fullest transcript of the notes so that my excellent friend, your chairman, may form a case to present to the House of Commons. Recollect, good people, that you are vindicating your dearest right, trial by jury. I will always stand up, cheerfully and boldly, for the welfare, happiness and independence of all classes in England and I now move a resolution: "That the evidence published in the newspapers charges the Metropolitan Police with violently assaulting a peaceable meeting of the people on Monday, the 13th May; and if that evidence shall not be contradicted, such conduct will not only merit public indignation, but affords an indisputable proof that the police force, as at present directed, is at variance with the peace and welfare of the country".'

A Mr D. Wakefield briefly seconded the resolution.

Mr Henry Hunt, who had put in an appearance at the inquest and was restrained by the coroner, now rose to speak. The

Another Political Meeting

Observer, which reported the meeting, describes his performance so well that it is quoted verbatim.

'Mr Hunt rose, and commenced a very long harangue which for the sake of himself, for the sake of the society to which it was addressed and, though last not least, for our own sakes, we shall not publish. He commenced by the tale *decies repetita* of his own conduct and prophecies for many years past and, after a long vagrancy in egotism, vomited forth some very foolish advice about self-defence. He then proceeded to attack Mr Roebuck and Mr O'Connell for not having roused the House of Commons on the subject stating that, had he been there, he would have soon caused an investigation into the whole affair. (Cheers and derisive laughter).'

The chairman explained his inability to raise the matter in the House before but expressed his intention of doing so a few days thence. Mr Hunt, who must have been a terrible bore, then resumed his remarks but wandered so far from the object of the meeting that the chairman said that he had given Mr Hunt every latitude but must now ask him to keep to the point. The *Observer* relates:—

'Mr Hunt, in high dudgeon, sat down but immediately afterwards rose and descended the platform. When on the point of quitting the room, and apparently out of the reach of harm, the worthy Ex valiantly turned round and with Stentorian lungs called out "I never saw so foul a chairman in my life" and at once disappeared.'

The resolution was then put to the meeting and carried. A second resolution was then put and also carried with acclaim.

'That this meeting contemplate with the greatest satisfaction the conduct of the coroner's jury on the Calthorpe Street affair and regard it as highly creditable to them as Englishmen, the verdict being a just recognition of the ancient and undoubted right to resist any forcible and illegal interference with any peaceable assemblage of the people.'

'That the sanction given by persons acting in the name of some members of the Government to the late outrageous attack on the people—the proclaiming that to be murder which the jury decided to be justifiable homicide—and the apprehension that advantage may have been taken of technical defects in the verdict to mitigate its effect—convinces this meeting that the Ministry are the inveterate enemies of liberal principles, and afford additional reasons for their no longer retaining the respect and confidence of the people.'

The meeting then subscribed money to assist the defence of those persons who were awaiting trial for charges arising out of the Calthorpe Street affair. The meeting broke up quietly at about half past eleven.

XV

The Trial of George Fursey

The meeting at the Crown and Anchor, presided over by John Roebuck, M.P., was one of many but is worthy of full treatment because it was better organized than most and because the speakers were experienced and able to put their case coherently. The egregious Henry Hunt took the chair at another meeting, chiefly noteworthy for scurrilous remarks about the police and those who testified in their favour. At Hunt's meeting the petition to Parliament on June 7th was concocted. There were many smaller meetings, mostly for the purpose of applauding the inquest verdict and collecting funds for the assistance of those in custody who faced prosecution.

The liberal newspapers, the *Morning Advertiser,* the *True Sun, Bell's Weekly Despatch* and *Bell's New Weekly Messenger* gave most of these gatherings coverage, but *The Times* preserved an aloof silence, except for the trial of George Fursey. After more than a century it is impossible to assess the reactions of the average citizen to the Cold Bath Fields affray. To read the radical newspapers is to form an impression that the institution of trial by jury had been violently suppressed by the wicked law officers of a Government bent on dictatorship. The truth was that the jury's verdict was quite perverse, but also that the Solicitor-General had been a little unwise in his method of quashing it. The radicals were an irresponsible minority at that time—Lord Melbourne and the Commissioners were, after all, responsible for the lives and property of those who lived in the Metropolis.

Nevertheless, it appears that authority was anxious to show itself in a milder light. On Tuesday, May 28, 1833, at Bow Street Magistrates' Court, Charles Wheeler, Official of the Society for

The Clerkenwell Riot

Suppressing Cruelty to Animals, charged Police Constable 32 A, John Graham, with assault. Wheeler repeated the evidence he had given at the inquest and once more produced his bloodstained clothing. He showed his head, which was now wrapped in bandages. An official of a rival animal protection organization also gave evidence but was so diffuse, rambling and prejudiced that he was of little help. The court was packed, a number of senior police officers were present and the hearing was prolonged. Police Constable Graham was committed for trial at the Court of King's Bench, he was allowed bail in the sum of £40. Mee, who had been charged with conducting an illegal meeting, had found two sympathizers to put up his bail money and was released.

On Thursday, May 30th, four men were brought from detention before Sir Frederic Roe. They were Hobbs and Roome, who had thrown stones at police from St Andrew's burial ground, and two men named Foley and Taylor. These men had been held in custody for seventeen days by now. Sir Frederic informed them that the law officers did not intend to proceed with the prosecution and they were discharged.

Careful perusal of the Daily Police Report of the time fails to disclose any prosecution other than that of Fursey arising from the Cold Bath Fields meeting. Every charge made at Bow Street, down to the most minor larceny, was recorded in the Daily Police Report. Current newspaper reports give no information of proceedings against others who were arrested at the time of the affray. Prosecution of Mee, for unlawful assembly, or of Lee for treasonable utterance must have received considerable attention. No doubt the law officers realized that parade of Lee's foolish remark about taking off the King's head as a treasonable utterance would be sufficiently farcical to play into the hands of their political opponents. It is probable that by now the Government regretted breaking up the meeting at Cold Bath Fields and were in a mind to play the whole thing down. The only conclusion to be drawn is that all the prisoners other than Fursey were quietly released with a minimum of fuss.

On July 4, 1833 George Fursey stood trial at the Old Bailey charged with stabbing John Brook in Calthorpe Street on May 13, 1833 with intent to do him grievous bodily harm. Other counts on which he was charged arose from the same incident and were not proceeded with. Mr Justice Gaselee presided, sitting with

The Trial of George Fursey

Mr Justice Parke, Mr Recorder Law and the Lord Mayor. Naturally this trial attracted much attention and several legal principles were laid down during its progress. There are full technical accounts in the law reports of the day.[1] This was held to be a state trial and the Solicitor-General, instructed by the Treasury Solicitor, led for the prosecution. Opening, the Solicitor-General said that as the prisoner's counsel had no power to address the jury and as he did not believe that one side should have a privilege not possessed by the other, he would make no statement of the facts, but would leave them to be given by the witnesses.

The main witness, Brooks had resigned from the Metropolitan Police on June 2nd as a result of his wound. In various accounts his name is given as Brooks, Brooke or Brook. As a police sergeant he had been paid 22s 6d a week and wellwishers had contributed sums of money for him of which he had been allowed to keep £5. Brooks stated that he was then in the North Lincoln Militia as a sergeant-major. He described how he went out into Calthorpe Street with C division and saw large numbers of people there. He caught sight of the prisoner, Fursey, who was carrying an American flag: before Brooks had time to raise his staff or strike anyone Fursey attacked him with a brass-hilted dagger. He received a severe blow in the left side which proved, fortunately, to have struck his sixth rib. Shortly after the injury he found himself unable to see clearly—'My sight was taken away.' Before this occurred he saw Redwood scuffling with Fursey. Brooks never saw the meeting proper or the hustings. He did not think people were trying to get away, rather did they appear to be advancing on his division, with intent to drive them out of the street. The people were not peaceable but Brooks could not swear there was no act of violence until he was stabbed.

Mr Phillips, counsel for Fursey, said he wished to make it clear that this was a Government prosecution and that all the power of Government was against the poor prisoner. Gaselee observed that no one doubted this and that the Solicitor-General had acted with the greatest fairness and liberality in refusing to open with a statement to the jury.

The question as to whether police were present in plain clothes, so that the people could not recognize that they were there

[1] Rv Fursey [1833] State trials, new series, 3 543: 6 Carrington & Payne 81.

as constables, was then raised. Brooks was asked whether he knew a man called Popay, the police spy who has already been mentioned as the cause of a Committee of Inquiry on police spying. Popay was brought into court but Brooks was unable to recognize him. Brooks said he had been twenty-five years in the first Grenadier Guards and was present at the battle of Waterloo. After he was stabbed he saw the prisoner in the coach house. Fursey was called out by name and Brooks was immediately able to identify him; that was about an hour and a half after he was stabbed.

Another count on the indictment of Fursey was for stabbing Police Constable Redwood. Giving evidence, Redwood described how Brooks, his sergeant, had ordered Fursey to give up the American flag. He then heard Brooks cry 'Oh!' and Fursey passed him. Immediately Redwood grasped the flag with both hands and received a stab through the forearm. He struck Fursey on the head and collared him.

At this point the Solicitor-General asked Redwood the nature of his wound. Objection was taken to the question as it was the subject of a separate charge from the wounding of Brooks. After consultation with his brother Judge, Gaselee, J., allowed the question as tending to assist the identification of a weapon in the possession of the prisoner. Redwood said his wound was three-sided. Redwood stated he had handed the prisoner over to Constables Compton and Holland. He said that all this time people were shouting and hallooing and that stones and brickbats were flying.

Mr Phillips then assailed Redwood's credibility by asking about a charge of assault which Redwood had been required to answer some years before. He also referred to a complicated matter in connexion with the ownership of a watch, alleged to have been stolen, which Redwood had given to his wife. Redwood said that he had bought the watch in a regular manner.

Police Constable Compton, of C division, was close to Redwood in Calthorpe Street, and heard him say he was stabbed but did not actually see the wound inflicted. At that time Redwood had hold of the prisoner. Compton went to his assistance and with the aid of Police Constable Holland took Fursey to Busbridge's stables. Police and the mob were struggling together and blows were struck on both sides. Stones flew and he saw a man hit with a

The Trial of George Fursey

short stick loaded with lead. Compton only stayed in the stables with Fursey for about two minutes. Blood was running down Fursey's forehead. At this time Fursey was not searched and there was only one other prisoner in the stable. Compton returned to his division: he stated that he did not see men, women and children who had been smashed. If it had been done in Calthorpe Street he must have seen it.

Police Constable Holland also heard Redwood exclaim he was stabbed and he seized hold of Fursey. No one had searched Fursey for a weapon. Police Constable Hales recounted that he was in Busbridge's stables and put a truss of straw into a stall. There was a good light and he was absolutely certain that no weapon was on the floor of the stall when he put in the straw. Only after Fursey and Tilley had been in the stable had he noticed some kind of pamphlet in the straw; searching more closely he found under the straw a dagger, pistol and powder flask. These he produced in Court. There was no blood on the dagger, which was in a sheath when he found it.

Sergeant Brooks was recalled: after examining the dagger he said he had seen one like it in Fursey's hand but he could not swear it was the same one. Fursey had a close-bodied coat, not one with large pockets into which he might have put the dagger. Redwood also said he could not swear that the dagger with which he had been struck was the one produced, but it was very like it.

Mr W. Fisher said 'I am a surgeon. I attended Brooks on the 13th of May. He had received a wound over the sixth rib on the left side. I probed the wound. The blow must have been given with some violence and the instrument had stuck in the rib. In all probability, had the instrument not been stopped, it would have passed the heart. I examined Redwood the following morning. He had a wound of a triangular form on the left arm. Such a wound might have been inflicted by such an instrument as the one produced.'

This closed the case for the prosecution. There was clear evidence of the stabbing, the prisoner was arrested on the spot and the chain of events to the stable was unbroken. A dagger similar to the one with which Brooks and Redwood had been wounded was found under the straw in the stable where Fursey had been confined. The prisoner then said his feelings were so overpowered that he would not attempt to make any defence, but would leave the jury to judge from the evidence of his own witnesses.

Nathaniel Stallwood was the first defence witness. He repeated what he had said at the inquest and said that from his balcony he could see 700 to 800 police assembled. After the Gough Street detachment had been ordered to charge, the ground was immediately strewn with the bodies of victims. The outrage continued for an hour and a half before the place was cleared. The police did not appear to be under any control whatever and, in fact, some of them appeared to be drunk.

His credibility was attacked by the Solicitor-General and he answered

'Yes, I was in the commission of the peace but I was superseded, by what means I cannot say. I am still a member of the select vestry. In 1819 or 1820 I was charged at the quarter sessions for assaulting a boy who had thrown some glass bottles on my premises, and fined ten pounds. I was at that time spending my private fortune in building speculation. I was brought up as an architect. I did not leave off speculating until I had realized £40,000 or £50,0000.

'I knew nothing of this meeting until I read a notice on the prison walls, which I did not consider a proclamation as it was not signed. The notice was a caution for persons not to attend a meeting to be held the following day. The notice was for holding a national meeting or convention as the only means for securing the rights of the people.' Mr Phillips, for Fursey, 'My Lord, I object to this mode of examination. My learned friend has the document before him and, as this is a Government prosecution, I cannot conceive why this printed notice has not been put in and read.'

The placard was produced and shown to the witness, who declared it was a true copy of the one he saw and it was then read by the Clerk of Arraigns.

Stallwood—'I thought that the document, as it did not specify which Secretary of State, ought to be disregarded. I never

The Trial of George Fursey

considered whether the meeting was or was not illegal. A meeting held by Mr O'Connell had ten times the number and the people dispersed quietly. All the flags at Cold Bath Fields have been displayed elsewhere, and more too. The American flag on the table was unfurled all the way down the street but I think the person who carried it rolled it up as he approached the hustings. I despised the meeting myself. I cannot recognize Fursey, or Brooks, or Redwood.'

Stallwood was re-examined by Mr Phillips—'There are four Secretaries of State. I consider the placard a "puff". I was made a magistrate under the present Government. I was a reformer from birth and am so to the present moment. I have been superseded by the present Government, who refuse to tell me why. If I had had half a dozen policemen I could have taken every one of those persons into custody.'

J. M. A. Courtney, of the *Courier*, next gave evidence. His testimony was similar to that given at the inquest and he emphasized the impossibility of members of the crowd escaping and the brutality practised by the police.

'The police appeared to be under no control than that of the worst of passions. I saw two policemen striking a woman. The attack was made on the people before the police came near the banner. The attack was frightful—it was appalling. In my judgment there would have been no difficulty in dispersing the meeting if the police had been so disposed.'

The Reverend Mr Pearson, Minister of Bunhill Fields Chapel and John Hudson, a hairdresser of Little Guilford Street, both described incidents of persons being struck by police with batons. Hudson said he had been belaboured by police, whom he considered to have been drunk.

Cross-examined by the Solicitor-General Hudson said that he did not know the meaning of the words 'national convention' as the only means of securing the rights of the people. 'I would not have attended a meeting to put down the Lords and Commons. I went to the meeting for the purpose of finding out what a national convention meant. I saw Fursey with the banner and a number of police struggling with him to get it away. Fursey was struck repeatedly on the head. I saw ten or twelve policemen who were so drunk that they could scarcely make a walk of it. Redwood's manner was the most outrageous and violent.'

Several more witnesses followed, all of whom gave examples of police brutality. Much of the testimony was in the most highly coloured terms and it is perfectly obvious that there was much exaggeration, if not downright perjury. After the witnesses of fact a succession of respectable tradesmen gave Fursey, the prisoner, a most exemplary character for humanity, honesty, mildness of disposition and general urbanity of manners. Some of these witnesses to character had known him from boyhood.

After some legal argument by the defence the Solicitor-General claimed the right to recall Redwood. Redwood said that he was sober, as were all the men of his division. He struck no one until he was stabbed and only struck Fursey once.

The defence made no attempt to deny that Fursey stabbed the policemen and were relying on the abundant evidence of provocation by the police. Mr Justice Gaselee began his summing up at five minutes to eleven at night. Most of the jurors had already made up their minds and twice informed his Lordship that they did not wish to trouble him, but on each occasion one juror expressed the desire that he should proceed.

The Judge went into great detail and was scrupulously fair. The first thing to be decided was whether the meeting was legal or illegal. If it was a legal meeting the officer was not entitled to take away the flag. If the meeting was legal, was the provocation sufficient to justify the prisoner in striking with such a deadly weapon? It made a difference whether a man took up such a weapon on the sudden or whether he went with it and was prepared to use it. If he took the weapon with the intention to resist the taking away of the flag, and if death ensued, he would have committed murder. Was there sufficient provocation, that had he killed the crime could be reduced to manslaughter?

The Judge's observations on unlawful assembly have been reported and are still quoted as authority in legal textbooks. On the question of the proclamation in the Riot Act he mentioned that the law had been laid down by the Judges on the special commissions and that it was clear that a riot is not the less a riot, nor is an illegal meeting the less an illegal meeting, because

The Trial of George Fursey

the proclamation from the Riot Act has not been read. The effect of that proclamation is to make the parties guilty of a capital offence if they do not disperse within an hour; but if that proclamation be not read, the parties are guilty of the common law offence, which is a misdemeanour, and all magistrates, constables and even private individuals are justified in dispersing the offenders, and if they cannot otherwise succeed in doing so, they may use force. Without any proclamation at all be a meeting illegal, a party attending it, knowing it to be so, is guilty of an offence.

Referring to the meeting at Cold Bath Fields 'to adopt measures for holding a national convention as the *only* means of securing the rights of the people' was an illegal purpose. The Judge held that the meeting was an illegal meeting.

The Government warning notice had little import other than to draw the attention of those who might attend to this illegality.

Mr Justice Gaselee concluded a summing up of two and a quarter hours by observing that on behalf of the prisoner it was shown that the conduct of the policemen was very violent and very dangerous. Was their conduct a sufficient provocation to the prisoner to resist? The jury had two questions to answer. Did the prisoner wound Brooks? Was there provocation of a kind which would reduce murder to manslaughter? If he had prepared the weapon with a view to protecting the flag under all circumstances the crime would not be so reduced. His Lordship felt that it did not appear to him that such a circumstance had been shown.

The jury retired at ten minutes past one in the early morning. When they returned at twenty minutes past two the foreman said 'My Lords, we have, as your Lordships are aware, given not only long but close and anxious attention to this case, and have since we retired considered, with all the care which it was possible to bring to bear upon it, the evidence on both sides, and we cannot on such evidence conscientiously pronounce any other verdict than not guilty.'

During the hearing large numbers of people thronged the yard of the Old Bailey and the surrounding streets. By about eleven o'clock the crowd thinned out, as many thought the trial could not possibly end before morning. Although there were groups of twenty or thirty persons each who were obviously members of

Trades' Unions, by midnight only the immediate friends of the accused man lingered. The Court room itself was packed and when the verdict was returned there was a roar of applause which was quickly taken up in the narrow streets until it seemed impossible that they could contain the sound.

The verdict followed that of the inquest: widespread hostility to the police found expression in wildly exaggerated evidence of the witnesses for Fursey. It could not be denied that the police took a rough line but nobody seemed to remember that they were dealing with a number of very ugly characters, as the stabbings showed. Provocation there may have been, there was also retaliation—of a dangerous and fatal nature. Probably the verdict was in the public interest; had Fursey gone to the scaffold or to prison he would have become a martyr.

In the light of Fursey's acquittal it would have been interesting to learn what a jury would have made of the charge of assault against P.C. 32 A, John Graham. Would he have been found to have acted in the course of duty? Or would he have been found guilty of assaulting Charles Wheeler? The Judge had said that any party attending an illegal meeting, knowing it to be so, is guilty of an offence. There is no record of Graham having appeared before the Court of King's Bench. The trial of Fursey was the last legal proceeding to arise out of the Cold Bath Fields affray.

A few days after Fursey's discharge it was reported that a public dinner would be given in his honour at the Sawyers Arms, George Street, Camberwell. Mr Benjamin Hawes, M.P., of the Old Barge House, Lambeth, wrote to the Commissioner asking for his observations about a report that the landlord of the Sawyers Arms, Woodford, had assaulted a Union Hall officer (the precursor of the modern court warrant officer). Had Superintendent McLean, of Camberwell, instigated a premediated prosecution of Woodford saying that he would 'do away with Woodford altogether?'

The Superintendent denied the allegation. He asked the Commissioner for instructions for action in the event of a disturbance at the Sawyers Arms on the night of the dinner for Fursey. The house might be open late and the Superintendent thought police interference might be misinterpreted. He was directed that

The Trial of George Fursey

there was to be no interference unless there was a breach of the peace in the streets.

On Tuesday, July 30, 1833 the National Union of the Working Classes met at White Conduit House, Clerkenwell, to celebrate the second French revolution. George Fursey was present.

XVI

Celebrations

Never before or since in the history of our country has a jury been feted in such a way. It seemed as though part of the population was temporarily bereft of its senses. Coming at a time when the Reform Act of 1832 had disappointed many, the verdict was regarded as a noble stand against official tyranny. The quashing of the verdict was seen as a downright assault on the jury system; nobody seemed to reflect that verdicts have been set aside on appeal time and time again. It appeared that all the traditional rights of the people had been attacked at the time of Cold Bath Fields, the meagre extension of the electoral franchise had led to the belief that a National Convention might in truth be the only means of securing the rights of the people, the right to freedom of speech had been suppressed by police, a coroner had attempted to impose a verdict on a jury against its will and, now, their valiant verdict had been quashed by the High Court.

Men who stoutly upheld the Englishman's freedom, however wrongheadedly, deserved reward and appreciation. However, it is proper to observe that the junketings were arranged by a small, though noisy, group who were prepared blithely to ignore the principles of justice for their own ends. This midsummer madness did not last long.

The River Thames has always been a favourite scene for Londoners' pleasurable outings. Monday, July 8, 1833 was greeted by a pouring wet morning but the bad weather in no way damped the enthusiasm of crowds of people who gathered at Blackfriars to salute the heroes of the hour, the Culley inquest jury. The jurors and their families were to be taken on the steam-packet *Endeavour* to Richmond and Twickenham. The excursion was arranged by the Milton Street Committee, a group of City

Celebrations

men with radical leanings. As the party assembled every juror was presented with a silver medal in commemoration of the verdict. As they proceeded upstream the boat was vociferously cheered from the banks and from the bridges. Most of the members of the party sheltered from the rain below decks, to the disappointment of the sightseers. The gaiety of the occasion was enhanced by a band, by songs, drinking and speeches.

It was still raining when the *Endeavour* reached Twickenham but crowds of people thronged the landing stage and a marquee had been erected in the garden of the inn. As the boat drew to the landing stage an irregular salute of five or six six-pounder cannon startled the ladies, set dogs barking and produced clouds of sulphurous smoke. Mr Mackenzie of the Milton Street Committee took the chair at a lavish dinner to which about eighty sat down. The side of the tent was open to provide a pleasant view of the River. Afterwards there were many prolonged speeches and toasts, including one to the jury which acquitted George Fursey. Early in the afternoon the weather improved and the ladies insisted on dancing on the green. The return journey down river was passed with music and singing in the evening sunshine.

Of the various committees who exerted themselves on behalf of the jurors and others implicated in the Calthorpe Street fracas that of the Milton Street group was by far the most active. On Monday, July 15th they organized an outing to the New London Bridge Theatre where the jurors and their families were entertained by a performance of *A Rowland for an Oliver*. The audience applauded the jury as much as they did the actors.

A few days after the notorious verdict a heavy parcel was delivered at the home of Samuel Radness Stockton, the foreman. It contained a number of medallions of an alloy similar to pewter. The donor, who was anonymous, enclosed a note requesting Mr Stockton to keep half a dozen for himself and to arrange for a similar number to be given to the other jurymen. One of these medallions is to be seen in the London Museum. It is about one-and-three-quarter-inches in diameter, on the obverse the circumference bears the words 'We shall be recompensed at the resurrection of the just' in relief around the jurors' names. On the reverse is stamped 'In honour of men who nobly withstood the dictation of a coroner; and by the judicious, independent and conscientious discharge of their duty; promoted a continued reliance upon the laws under the protection of a British Jury.'

On Friday, July 26, 1833 an advertisement on the front page of the *Morning Advertiser* announced that on Monday, July 29th the *Royal Sovereign*, commanded by Captain R. Grant, would leave St Katharine's Dock at eight o'clock for Rochester on an excursion, the object of which was to raise money for a monument to commemorate the glorious verdict of the inquest jury. In an inside column of the *Advertiser* it was reported that the Milton Street Committee had already decided the nature of the monument, which was to be a column of cast iron, suitably inscribed to the everlasting glory of the gallant jury. Although it was rumoured that designs were under consideration there is no record of this phallic memorial being completed.

The columnist wrote that the jury would assemble at the Calthorpe Arms and then make a triumphal progress to St Katharine's Dock. The order of the procession was given

Small flag

Band

Large banner

JURY
with white rosettes and medals

Committee
with blue rosettes and medals

Milton Committee
with blue rosettes

There is a distinct impression that somebody was deriving intense satisfaction from making these detailed arrangements.

The banner was a truly magnificent production, which is now to be seen above a staircase in the London Museum. A contemporary description in the most precious terms faces it. The banner has been skilfully restored but some of the original inscriptions are missing. Funds for making the banner and the general arrangements were organized by Mr Ritchie, the landlord of the Marquess Wellesley, in Cromer Street, Gray's Inn Lane.

Celebrations

It was designed, gratuitously, by Mr Wight, an artist of Cromer Street and the gold lettering was done free of charge by a local craftsman.

The banner is of blue silk, ten feet by eight. The centre is a life sized portrait of Samuel Stockton, the foreman of the jury, within a border inscribed 'Calthorpe Jury'. This is surrounded by a wreath of oak leaves and a circle of smaller medallion portraits of the other jurymen. Considering the speed with which the banner and portraits were made, it was said that the likenesses were good. At the top of the banner are seventeen stars and a draped female Britannia, with a symbolic figure of Fame to the left and Freedom to the right. The lower part of the banner is occupied with a convoluted riband bearing the inscription on large letters 'Britain's Bulwark. Trial by Jury'. Hanging from the riband is a pendant medallion which originally bore the words of the verdict and the motto '*Salus populi suprema lex*'. The general effect is very striking and a visit to the London Museum to inspect it is recommended.

At 6.30 a.m. on the great day the jury, with their families and friends, assembled at the Calthorpe Arms. The banner started out from the Marquess Wellesley about half a mile up the Gray's Inn Lane. The weather was perfect and the whole excursion took place beneath a cloudless sky. Twelve open landaus were provided and the band travelled in a coach. The cortege took the announced order and, as ever, despite the early hour, there was no dearth of onlookers. The procession moved off at seven o'clock with the band playing, flags flying and the banner swaying to the movement of its bearers. Hundreds joined the procession which made its way through Gray's Inn Lane, Mount Pleasant Street, St John Street and Barbican to Milton Street, where the Committee awaited its arrival at the Jacob's Head. Reinforced by their sponsors and by liquid refreshment the party continued to St Katharine's Dock where, unimpeded by the crowds of sightseeers, the members of the outing embarked on the *Royal Sovereign* without mishap.

About 500 people were on board and the band played merrily as they steamed down the river. Many danced throughout the day and there was much laughter and song. For the more serious minded there were improving speeches on the right to trial by jury and the iniquities of those who tried to curtail this funda-

The Clerkenwell Riot

mental safeguard of the people. Mr Samuel Stockton exercised his growing talent for oratory, there were many toasts and a well-nigh interminable discourse on the history of the development of the English jury system. There were so many people to feed that three dinners were served, and here one tiny cloud marred the merrymaking. Next day the *Morning Advertiser* reluctantly noted 'we regret to say that the dinner did not give satisfaction, either as to quantity or quality, but it is right to add that the Captain threw the entire blame on his butcher.' It is to be hoped that there was a sufficiency of liquor to enable the audiences to endure with fortitude the punishing speeches with which they were assailed. However, the general opinion was that the outing was a success and the *Royal Sovereign* returned to London at a late hour, having voyaged almost to Rochester Bridge.

A year after the inquest an anniversary banquet was given by the Friends of Trial by Jury on May 21, 1834 at the Highbury Barn Tavern. Although Sir Samuel Whalley M.P. took the chair it was noted that only two Members of Parliament were present. About 150 sat down to dinner at five o'clock. The banquet was fully reported by the *True Sun* which repeatedly referred to the 'Cold Bath Fields Outrage', and by the *Morning Advertiser*. *The Times* did not mention it at all. While the general tone was that of hilarious celebration rather than serious political intention there was, all the same, a noticeably radical atmosphere. The loyal toasts were observed but drunk with a complete lack of enthusiasm, after which an entertainer revived the spirits of the gathering. The *Advertiser* noted 'Mr Buckingham, after the loyal toasts, sang a comic song which was received with loud laughter, he then gave imitations of character which were remarkably characteristic and called forth loud and universal applause.'

The announcement of the main toast 'The people, the only source of legitimate power' produced thunderous acclamation. Mr Mackenzie, chairman of the Milton Street Committee, referred at length to the determination of the English people to resist oppression and to the courage of gallant jurymen in withstanding the blandishments of the authorities. He blamed the Government for sending police to suppress an innocent meeting with the inevitable result which they all knew. At the end of Mr Mackenzie's speech other members of the Milton Street Committee were seen leaving the room. They soon returned bringing with them seven-

Celebrations

teen silver cups. One juror was unable to attend owing to illness but the other sixteen were called up to the chairman one by one, congratulated and presented with a cup.

The cup given to Samuel Stockton is now in the London Museum. It is of goblet form about six inches high and three and a half inches in diameter. At the junction of stem and cup it is ornamented with some scroll work. The inscription reads:—

'This cup was presented on 20th of May, 1834 by the Milton Street Committee, City of London, to Mr Samuel Stockton, foreman of the memorable Calthorpe Street inquest jury as a perpetual memorial of their glorious verdict of Justifiable Homicide on the body of Robert Culley, a policeman, who was slain, while brutally attacking the people when peaceably assembled in Calthorpe Street on the 13 May, 1833.

Alexander Mackenzie, Chairman
G. Webb & J. Nicholson, Trustees
Thos Reynolds, Secretary.

Stockton, on behalf of the jury, expressed their most warm thanks. In the past year his memory of the truth that the people were not prevented by the police from escaping had completely vanished but he had acquired a little knowledge of the law, probably from the oft-repeated utterances of Mr O'Connell and his friends. He said 'Every authority says that if a man be attacked and driven to the wall and death ensues it shall be justifiable homicide. The crowd could not retreat because they were assailed from all four directions. Being driven to the wall they had the undoubted right of repelling force by force.' He spoke angrily of quashing of the inquest verdict with its implication of bias and lack of integrity; referring to Lord Melbourne he remarked. 'I throw back the implication of perjury in his Lordship's teeth with all the contempt, scorn and indignation which I regret the want of language to express.' He renewed his thanks to those present as being the true friends of the people and sat down amidst applause.

Two others jurors, Graham and Pearson, also spoke. They stated that they had received thousands of letters of approbation and pointed out that the members of the jury were by no means indigent but that they had a stake in the maintenance of law and the protection of property. 'One or two of us have considerable property—we all have some.'

The chairman, Sir Samuel Whalley M.P., referred to the forbearance of the Government in allowing a peaceable passage to a Trades Union procession through the Metropolis, which he ascribed to the stand made by the Calthorpe Street jury. He spoke scathingly of the Government and police saying that they had set up 'a newly-created power, in the shape of a Metropolitan police force at its back—a power looked upon by the masses with great distrust; viewed, as it naturally was, as a military organization in the hands of the Government to stifle the public voice.' He added many encomiums of Stockton and the jury and praised them with reference to the recent Trades Union procession '... to that verdict Englismen were to ascribe the fact that the streets did not on that day stream with blood. Nay, more, it had saved the Government from the guilt of slaughtering their fellow subjects!'

These were wonderful, sonorous, distorted and untrue words. Not a word of pity for Robert Culley or of sympathy for his widow. Not a suggestion that the verdict was a perverse one, nor any admission that the whole of Cold Bath Fields and the pavements of Calthorpe Street were available to the crowd for dispersal, no recognition that Robert Culley, far from brutally attacking the people, was never seen to strike anybody.

There was yet another presentation, the Editors of the *True Sun*, the *Morning Advertiser*, *Bell's Weekly Despatch* and *Bell's New Weekly Messenger* were given silver pens with an inscription

'Presented on 20th May, 1834 to the Editor of ......, advocate of trial by jury and defender of the verdict of Justifiable Homicide delivered on the 20th May, 1833 on the body of Robert Culley, a police soldier slain while brutally attacking the people in Calthorpe Street.'

The amount of speechmaking which the members of the jury had to sustain was some retribution, if slight, for their perverse verdict. The toast of the ladies was honoured and Mr Mackenzie was given the inevitable medal. A ball followed and the revellers danced long into the night.

Celebrations

Time passed, the Chartist disturbances came and went, Victoria came to the throne and the English people went to war in the Crimea and suffered the horrors of the Indian Mutiny. On March 5, 1861, forty or fifty ratepayers of St Pancras dined at the Argyle Tavern to honour Mr Samuel Radness Stockton and the Benevolent Institution which he represented as secretary. He was presented with a French drawing-room clock worth twenty guineas for his work for parish and poor for more than thirty years. During the recital of his many services and benefactions his sturdy captainship of the jury after the Cold Bath Fields affray was mentioned.

Four years later, in 1865, Stockton presented his many friends with a slim booklet which had been collated by Mr Charles Greene, of the *Observer* and the *Morning Advertiser*. The title page bears the noble wording 'Trial by Jury and Local Self-Government... showing the determination of an English jury, despite the blandishments and intimidation of the Government of the day, to deliver an honest verdict.' It commends Mr Samuel Radness Stockton, member of the vestry, churchwarden, strenuous defender of local rights and religious liberty.

After a short account of the benefits of trial by jury the book reproduces the various newspaper reports of the Culley inquest and the trial of Fursey. Opposite the title page is a photograph of Stockton in his later years. It is difficult to judge the age but he has a shrewd, calm, firm aspect. There is nothing of the fanatic or bigot nor is there great intellect, it is the face of a reasonable, prosperous tradesman, which is exactly what he was.

XVII

Assessment of the Affray

The Select Committee of the House of Commons appointed to inquire into the conduct of the police at Cold Bath Fields had a distinguished membership representative of all parties. It included Lord Althorp, Sir Robert Peel and Sir George Grey. The first meeting took place on July 18, 1833 and the Committee met subsequently on eight occasions. A remarkably full report was published on August 23, 1833, five weeks after the first meeting.

The Select Committee examined at length many of the witnesses who had given evidence at both the inquest on Culley and the trial of Fursey. As most of the testimony was repetitive it will only be necessary to mention evidence that had not been given before and to introduce four or five fresh witnesses, particularly Lord Melbourne.

Colonel Rowan was called early in the proceedings, he was received very courteously. As there was confusion as to the instructions which he had received from the Home Secretary he was examined at length on this topic. The Commissioner said he had received only verbal instructions from the Secretary of State. At the conference at the Home Office on May 11, 1833 he was told that the Cold Bath meeting was not to be allowed to take place but that, if it were attempted, it must be dispersed and the leaders seized. The Commissioner said that he had considered it inadvisable for police to occupy the ground beforehand.

Colonel Rowan went on to state that his orders to the police were given in writing. At the scene he had ordered out seventy to eighty men of A division, but only when he was satisfied that this was indeed the illegal meeting. Two support groups of a

Assessment of the Affray

hundred men each followed the seventy men of A division, one in Calthorpe Street and the other in Gough Street. These groups were not to play any active part unless A division was overwhelmed. Colonel Rowan was asked about the Riot Act. He explained its legal significance and said that he had taken a copy of the proclamation to Cold Bath Fields on the day of the affray. A member of the Select Committee asked him to read it out. He said that the Act requires a magistrate to approach as near to the rioters as he can safely come and with a loud voice to command silence and then to read the following proclamation

'Our sovereign lord the King chargeth and commandeth all persons, being assembled, immediately to disperse themselves and peaceably to depart to their habitations, or to their lawful business, upon the pains contained in the Act made in the first year of King George, for preventing tumults and riotous assemblies.
God save the King.'

An hour after this proclamation those who remain are liable for felony rather than the misdemeanour of unlawful assembly.

The Commissioner estimated that membership of the National Union of the Working Classes totalled about 3,000 in London, they were divided into local classes of 80 to 130. About 800 people were at Cold Bath Fields, he had 700 to 800 police but the dispersal was carried out by 70 men, with support. He knew in advance that many of the Union members would be armed. He was perfectly satisfied that none of his men had been drinking, for one thing they had no opportunity of leaving the stables until the fracas began. The dispersal took three to five minutes.

Reverting to the conference with Lord Melbourne on Saturday, May 11th, Colonel Rowan repeated that he had been instructed that the meeting must be dispersed. He adhered to this despite being told that Mr March Phillipps had said that no orders were given to disperse the meeting. The Commissioner knew nothing of the Government counter-notice until it was sent to him on the afternoon of May 11th. He distinctly recalled Lord Melbourne's words 'When the persons get up and talk about a National Convention you will know it is the illegal meeting announced by the placard.'

The Clerkenwell Riot

On May 27, 1833, after the fracas, Colonel Rowan had wanted to thank the police for their action in a police order of the day. Lord Melbourne had objected to this on the grounds that it might prejudice the trial of Fursey.

On August 8th Lord Melbourne himself appeared before the Select Committee; Sir George Grey was in the chair. He was asked to comment on a passage from a report of the Commissioners of Metropolitan Police.

'On Saturday the Commissioners received your Lordship's instruction that the meeting, being illegal, and public notice given to that effect, was not to be allowed to take place; that the meeting, if attempted, was to be dispersed, and the leaders seized on the spot; the police were to interfere for the purposes stated, the moment anyone began to address the meeting, but it was considered inadvisable to occupy the ground previously by the police.'

Sir George Grey—'My Lord, is that correct?'

Lord Melbourne—'From my recollection, I did not expressly direct the dispersion of the meeting; at the same time I conceive the instructions I had given to involve the necessity of not permitting the meeting to be held in pursuance of that placard.'

Sir George Grey—'Your Lordship intended that the police should confine their objects entirely to the arrest of persons attempting to hold the meeting—the ringleaders, and to the prevention of the meeting?'

Lord Melbourne—'Certainly. I thought the instructions were not quite accurately stated in this Report, at the same time, that they were correct in substance. The police were sent because of irregularity, not because a breach of the peace was anticipated. It is my custom always to give verbal instructions.'

It was clear that the Select Committee would get nothing more definite from Lord Melbourne. He was not prepared to assume responsibility for the dispersal of the meeting although he had indubitably caused a notice to be published to the effect that the meeting was illegal and that the civil authorities had strict orders to apprehend any persons offending therein. By no stretch of the imagination could Colonel Rowan have been considered to exceed these very plain instructions. Lord Melbourne said that

Assessment of the Affray

he had no doubt it was an illegal and dangerous meeting and that many present would be armed.

He was then asked about the Commissioners' desire to publish an order of the day appreciative of the police. Lord Melbourne —'I declined publication of the order of the day approving of the conduct of police because there were trials pending, not from any feeling of disapprobation of the police.'

The next part of the proceedings was occupied by Stallwood and his friends whose evidence was substantially similar to that given at the inquest and trial. Stallwood said he could have dispersed the meeting with half a dozen men and finished with the Parthian shot 'My opinion is that a great many of the police had drunk too much on that day, and that they appeared to me to be under no command whatever.' Various other witnesses added to the tales of police violence. One man had his hat knocked 100 yards, another said a policeman struck a pieman's tray and scattered the pies, a third said he was 'used shamefully'.

William Carpenter, the Editor of the *True Sun*, went to the preliminary meeting at the Union, in Bagnigge Wells Road at which six were present. Mee had said that the meeting would be dispersed by police and the leaders taken into custody. Mr Courtney, formerly of the *Courier*, and now of the *True Sun* spoke even more vehemently than Stallwood or Carpenter:

'I think the Minister and Governor of Police an assassin who arranged the approach of police on that day.' From Stallwood's balcony he had seen a man struck on the head as he was running away. With his colleague Mr Carpenter he protected 'an elderly woman who appeared to be pregnant and in great pain'.

Although many of the witnesses spoke of the way in which the police belaboured members of the public, and of the wounds they saw inflicted, it is surprising that none of the injured came forward to give evidence. One man, who said he saw some boys being beaten and that he took their names and addresses, had unfortunately mislaid the paper on which he wrote them.

James Brown, a surgeon, had examined Charles Wheeler, who brought a charge of assault against A 32 Police Constable Graham, and described three superficial scalp wounds, each one inch in length. Although the scalp notoriously bleeds freely, the suspicion that the lily of Wheeler's bloodstained clothing might have been gilded after a call at a slaughterhouse is irresistible. Another surgeon had attended two men for trivial bruises on their shoulders and a third for a mild lacerated wrist.

Mr John Nelson, a merchant, had stood on a doorstep on the corner of Gray's Inn Lane and Guilford Street. He watched the police column halt halfway up Calthorpe Street. The police occupied the carriageway only, leaving the sides free: he himself had passed freely up and down the pavements. He heard hissing but saw no violence. He saw no one struck but passed two men with blood on their heads. Mr Nelson saw no women at all.

Colonel de Roos thought it was a disreputable sort of mob and that the police had behaved with steadiness; he produced two Maceroni pikes which a gunsmith had said could be turned out by the dozen for about twopence apiece. Lieutenant Bulkeley, who thought it remarkable that only one of the prisoners was injured, heard a prisoner say 'You may take a few of us, but that is of no consequence; depend upon it some of you will lose your lives in this affray.'

Various members of the police spoke of their part in the affair. Superintendent Hunter expressed the view that Mr Stallwood was drunk. Another officer had been cut on the knuckles by a razor. Constable Angus, who had been struck in the mouth by Thomas Tilley, said that he was no longer in the force. The circumstances of his removal, in his own words, illustrate the severity with which the Commissioners treated even minor misbehaviour by police officers.

'There was a boy indecently exposing himself in Hyde Park and it was in some hollow trees; he was on the branch of a hollow tree, near to the Old Magazine; there were some ladies crossing the Park towards Kensington Gardens and this boy made use of some very indecent language; I went up and told the boy to come down and he would not; he made use of expressions, that I was a bloody Cold Bath's butcher; I broke a twig from one of the branches and climbed up to get him to come down; he went down the hollow into the bottom and I just struck him across the shoulders through his making use of those expressions and his irritating me as he had done; Mr White, the magistrate, in consequence of my striking him, said I had done wrong, and he

Assessment of the Affray

inflicted a penalty upon me and discharged the boy, and in consequence of that I was dismissed by the Commissioners.'

The published findings of the Select Committee of inquiry into the conduct of police at Cold Bath Fields were:
(1) No blame attaches to Commissioners for arrangements which they made for carrying out the instructions of the Secretary of State.
(2) The conduct of Police was not attended with greater violence than was occasioned by the resistance they met with from a portion of the meeting.
(3) That after the dispersion of the meeting some of the Police were suffered to follow persons to a greater distance than was necessary and that under these circumstances they were not subjected to that efficient control which, in a moment of excitement and irritation, and after much provocation, could alone prevent individual instances of undue exercise of power.
(4) That the meeting was held with full knowledge on the part of the leaders that public notice had been given by the Government of its being considered illegal and that interference from the Police might be anticipated; and that resistance was contemplated and that, for the purpose of such resistance, offensive weapons of a dangerous nature were carried and used by some of the persons composing the meeting.
(5) Police did not interfere until they were satisfied of the nature of the meeting and advanced in two directions only, leaving the north and east free. Opportunity was given for any persons not taking an active part in the meeting to escape.
(6) None of the Police were intoxicated, no dangerous wound or permanent injury has been shown to have been inflicted by them on any individual, while on the other hand one of their own number was killed by a dagger and two others stabbed in the discharge of their duty.
(7) That, while it is the opinion of this Committee, that the conduct of the Police, as a body, on the occasion in question, affords no just ground of complaint, they feel it a duty to advert to the importance of the utmost caution and vigilance on the part of the Superintendents and other Officers of the Police, to check any approach to unnecessary violence among their men on all occasions, but more especially where large bodies of

The Clerkenwell Riot

them are employed in the prevention or suppression of disturbance, and the maintenance of the public peace.

Naturally many regarded the Select Committee's findings as whitewashing the police, but study of the affair in the round leaves no doubt that it was a fair and accurate appraisal.

The Cold Bath Fields meeting had little prospect of success. The organizers were obscure and maladroit and the uneducated supporters ready dupes for the agitator. Such a meeting inevitably attracted known ruffians who came for violence and loot. It was their presence, just as much as the dread of subversive activity, which led the Government to take firm action. While it now seems probable that overt suppression of free speech was potentially more harmful than the meeting, the Home Secretary with full information thought otherwise. Having formed this opinion, police action followed as a matter of course.

Lord Melbourne's instructions to Colonel Rowan were not crystal clear, but the Government placard left no doubt of his intentions. Melbourne overlooked the provocative effect of the arrests, how could the police have possibly seized the ringleaders without disorganizing the meeting? The Commissioner carried out a police operation with precision and skill. Very few of the public were injured and the main dispersal was effected with only seventy men. It is impossible to believe the exaggerated accounts which were given by some of the witnesses of police brutality. Colonel Rowan had no idea of the numbers who might attend the meeting, he knew that many would be armed. Once he cried havoc, rough action became inevitable.

Robert Culley's death, unfortunately, resulted from a hazard which police officers face on our behalf every day. Known criminals were present at Cold Bath Fields and a secret knife is easily used in a crowd. He was one of the earliest of many brave men who have died so that the public may be secure. The sad thing was that this unnecessary meeting was ever called. It is not the vociferous Mees and Lees who bring about social reform but the O'Connells and Roebucks, patient politicians who know their trade and the serpentine twists of Parliamentary strategy. William Wilberforce, another great reformer at the time, struggled for forty-five years for the abolition of slavery. Wilberforce met with determined opposition but succeeded in the end without recourse to violence or agitation. His Abolition Bill was

Assessment of the Affray

passed in July 1833, four days before his death, while the Cold Bath Fields affray was still the subject of inquiry.

No doubt the furore which followed was due to the coroner's mishandling of the case. The sole purpose of an inquest is the ascertainment of the cause of death and other considerations must not be allowed to creep into the inquiry. The inquest should be largely conducted by the coroner and jurors should only be allowed to ask questions through the coroner to clarify points in the evidence. At the Calthorpe Arms a number of angry men sat eye to eye in an overheated room without any supervision at all. Small wonder that a perverse verdict resulted. The jurors were not heroes at all, they were merely pigheaded men defying authority—but they should have been more tactfully handled. Gradually the echoes of the Cold Baths Fields affray died down, the ranting and the speeches ceased leaving nothing but the sobs of a pregnant young widow in her humble home.

SOURCES

Archbold—*Criminal Pleading, Evidence and Practice*. Sweet and Maxwell.
Browne, Douglas—*The Rise of Scotland Yard*. Harrap, 1956.
Gash, Norman—*Mr Secretary Peel*. Longmans, 1961.
Reith, Charles—*The Blind Eye and History*. Faber and Faber, 1952.
Reith, Charles—*A New Study of Police History*. Oliver and Boyd, 1938.
Reith, Charles—*A Short History of the British Police*. Oxford University Press, 1948.
Sweet, S. and others—*Jervis on Coroners*. First Edition, 1829.
Trevelyan, G. M.—*History of England*. Longmans, 1947.
Wade and Phillips—*Constitutional Law*. Longmans, 1960, 6th edition.
Dictionary of National Biography.
Encyclopedia Brittanica.
Special Commission on the Police—Parliamentary Papers 1833, vol. xiii.
Trial by Jury—collated by Charles Greene.
Rv Fursey [1833] 6 Carrington and Payne 81. 3 State Trials (new series) 543.
Papers in the London Museum, Public Record Office (HO/61/8 and HO/61/9) New Scotland Yard.

JOURNALS
All for the period 1833-4.

Annual Register, Gentlemen's Magazine, Morning Advertiser, Observer, Telegraph, Times, True Sun.

LIBRARIES

Author's Club.
British Museum Newspaper Library (Colindale).
Finsbury Public Library, House of Commons, Inner Temple, Merton Public Library, Westminster City Reference Library.

Index

A'Court, P.C. Samuel, 59; Inquest evidence, 123
Adams, Samuel, 25–27
Affray, Definition of, 41
Alexander, William (Juror), 69, 120–123
Althorp, Lord, 172
American War of Independence, 22, 25–28
Angus, P.C., 57, 176
Anti-Slavery Society, 146
Apsley House, 39
Argyle Tavern, The, 171
Arnold, Thomas, 102

Bagnigge Wells, 43
Bagnigge Wells Road (see Kings Cross Road)
Baker, Superintendent Thomas, 57, 78, 80, 82–84, 86, 89, 122, 123; evidence at Inquest, 73–76; further evidence, 85
Bedlam Asylum, 50
Bell's New Weekly Messenger, 153, 170
Bell's Weekly Despatch, 153, 170
Benevolent Institution, 171
Biddulph, Thomas Middleton, Inquest evidence, 99–101
Blackfriars Bridge, 50
Bliss, John (Juror), 69
Bow Street Magistrates' Court, 28, 62, 63, 153, 154
Bow Street Runners, 28–30

Brooks, Sergeant John, 62, 74, 77, 115, 154, 159, 161; injured in affray, 58; evidence at Bow Street, 66, 67; evidence at Inquest, 73–76; evidence at George Fursey trial, 155, 157
Brown, James, 175
Buckingham, Mr, 168
Bulkeley, Lt Thomas, 176; Inquest evidence, 100
Bunn, Richard, 64
Burgess, Joseph (Juror), 69
Busbridge, Mr, 70
Busbridge's Riding Stables, 44, 45, 52, 54–56, 58, 61–63, 70, 74, 78, 92, 99, 100, 141, 156, 157

Calf, William, 64
Calthorpe, Lord, 44
Calthorpe Arms, 44, 59–61, 68, 69, 71, 74, 80, 112, 117, 120, 127, 135, 166, 167, 179
Calthorpe Street, 44, 52–63, 70, 73–75, 77–81, 86, 87, 89, 92, 95, 98, 101, 109, 110, 112, 117, 119, 120, 123, 126, 127, 141, 151, 152, 154–157, 165, 169, 170, 173, 176
Carpenter, Mr William, 88, 175; Inquest evidence, 90, 91
Charing Cross, 38
Chartism, 20, 21, 39, 170
Chartist riots, 20

Chartists, National Convention, 20, 47, 76, 90, 138, 145, 146, 149, 164, 173
Clements Inspector, Bow Street evidence, 63
Clerkenwell Prison, 65
Cobbett, William, 22
Cold Bath Fields, 20, 31, 39, 69, 70, 73, 80, 85, 86, 89, 102, 111, 119, 126, 138, 140–150, 153, 154, 159, 161, 162, 164, 168, 170–174, 176–179; Police action prior to affray, 41–48; origin of name, 43; first signs of trouble, 51; police arrive, 52; the affray, 57–59; aftermath, 60–62; reward for apprehending Culley murderer, 67; Culley Inquest, 68–135; verdict appraisal, 136; George Fursey trial, 153–163; assessment, 172–179
Cold Bath Fields affray, Inquiry, 143, 172–174; Findings, 177–179
Cold Bath Prison, 44
Collingridge's Coach Works, 56, 92, 100
Collis, P.C. John, 57
Colquhoun, Mr (Magistrate), 28, 29
Compton, P.C., 58, 67, 156, 157
Corn Laws, Repeal of, 21
Courier, The, 85, 159, 175
Courtney, Mr J. M. A., 90, 159, 175; evidence at Inquest, 85–89
Crown & Anchor Tavern, Strand, 144, 153
Culley, P.C. Robert, 39, 58, 60, 61, 67, 68, 70, 71, 74, 78, 80, 81, 89, 95, 97, 101, 115, 117, 119–123, 125, 128–130, 136–138, 142, 164, 169–172, 178; dies from stab wound, 59; Inquest, 68–135; funeral, 105; George Fursey trial, 153–163

Daily Police Report, 67, 154
Danton, Georges Jacques, 22
Davey, William, 65, 66
Davies, William (Juror), 69
Dawson's Livery Stables, 44, 45, 52, 56, 57, 62, 73, 80
Defensive Instructions to the People, 93
Dennis, George (Juror), 69
de Roos, Colonel, Brigade Major, Cavalry Brigade, 52, 55, 99, 176; Inquest evidence, 91–94
Director of Public Prosecutions, 33
Doller, John (Juror), 69

Edwards, James, 65
Endeavour, 165
Everard, Mr Charles, Inquest evidence, 81, 82

Factory Acts, 21
Fawcett, P.C. Robert, 57, 122, 123
Fielding, Henry (Magistrate), 28, 29
Finsbury Square affray, 39
Fisher, Mr W., George Fursey trial evidence, 157
Flack, P.C., Thomas, 58, 59; Inquest evidence, 80–82
Foley, Mr, 154
Forrest, Mr, 65
Fouché, Joseph, 29
Fowler, Richard, Inquest evidence, 79
Fox, Charles James, 17; principles for representation of people, 20
Freedom of speech, reference to, 40
French, Robert, 69
French Republicans, 137
French Revolution, 22, 27, 28
French State Police, 29
Fricker, Mr, 121
Friends of Trial by Jury, anniversary banquet 168

Index

Fursey, George, 77, 78, 84, 115, 116, 126, 153, 162, 163, 165, 171, 172, 174; Bow Street proceedings, 63, 65–67; Trial, 154–161
Fursey, William, 61, 65

Gaselee, Mr Justice, 155, 156, 160, 161
George III, King, 21, 25
Globe, The, 149
Goody, P.C., Bow Street evidence, 62
Goore, William Henry, 133; evidence at Inquest, 102–104
Gordon Riots, 25, 27, 41
Gough Street, 44, 52, 55, 58, 60, 70, 81, 86, 87, 92, 93, 97, 100, 107, 115, 158, 173
Graham, John, 69, 169
Graham, P.C. John, 154, 162, 175
Grant, James, Inquest evidence, 89, 90
Grant, Captain R., 166
Grays Inn Road (formerly Grays Inn Lane), 44, 52, 55, 56, 61, 70, 73, 81, 82, 85, 86, 92, 100, 102, 112, 114, 116
Greene, Mr Charles, 171
Grey, Earl, 19, 22, 38
Grey, Sir George, 172, 174
Grimsell, Superintendent, 51
Gude, Mr, 122

Hales, P.C., 157; Bow Street evidence, 62–63
Halls, Mr (Magistrate), 62
Hamilton, Mary, 136, 137, 139; Inquest evidence, 118, 119
Hastie, Benjamin (Juror), 69
Hawes, Mr Benjamin, M.P., 162
Hewlett, J. C., 107
Hicks, George, Bow Street evidence, 65
Highbury Barn Tavern, 168
Hobbs, Mr, 65, 154
Holder, Edward (Juror), 69
Holland, P.C., 58, 67, 156, 157

Home Office, 34, 35, 65, 66, 91, 172
Hope, James, 107
House of Correction, 92, 106
Hudson, John, George Fursey trial evidence, 159, 160
Hunt, Henry, 117, 121, 153; addresses Crown & Anchor meeting, 150, 151
Hunter, Superintendent, 176
Hutchinson, James, 64

Jacobs Head, The, 167
Jeffery, Mr John, 125; Inquest evidence, 112–116
Jervis on Coroners, 129
Jessopp, Mr (Magistrate), 70
Johnston, George, 107
Jolly Gardeners, The, 50

Kent, Duchess of, 30
Kent, George Henry, Inquest evidence, 79, 80
Keys, Mr, 121
Kings Cross Road (formerly Bagnigge Wells Road), 44, 52, 54, 57, 61, 65, 87, 90, 98, 101, 175
Knott, P.C. Charles, 65

Lambeth Police Station, 51
Langran, Joseph (Juror), 69
Law, Mr Recorder, 155
Lee, Richard Egan, 70, 72, 104, 137, 138, 154, 178; Cold Bath affray part, 53, 54; evidence at Bow Street, 64
Lincoln's Inn Fields, 55
Liverpool, Lord, 29
London Museum, 165–167
Lord Mayor of London, 155
Louis XVI, King, 22
Lucan, Lord 35
Lygon Colonel, 100

Maceroni, Colonel, 50, 93
Maceroni pike, 50, 57, 122, 176
Mackenzie, Mr Alexander, 165, 168–170
McLean, Superintendent, 162

McReath, James, 58
McWilliam, Mr (Magistrate), 70
Mallalieu, Inspector, 144
Marat, Jean Paul, 22
Marie Antoinette, Queen, 22
Markwood, P.C., 64
Marquess Wellesley, The, 166, 167
Mason, Mr, 141
May, Superintendent John, 55, 56, 61
Mayne, Mr Richard, 38, 75, 85, 105, 122; appointed Police Commissioner, 30; background of, 32; actions prior to Cold Bath affray, 43, 45, 48
Mee, Mr, 64, 70, 86, 103, 104, 112, 137, 138, 141, 144, 154, 175, 178; Lee proposes as chairman of meeting, 53; Cold Bath affray part, 54, 56, 57
Melbourne, Lord, 30, 38, 39, 48, 67, 85, 102, 105, 122, 140, 153, 169, 172–175, 178; conference prior to Cold Bath affray, 45; warning notice, 47
Metropolitan Police, 30, 33–35, 38, 39, 45, 55, 170
Metropolitan Police Bill, 29, 30, 38
Milton Street Committee, 164–166, 168, 169
Mines Act, 21
Minshell, Mr (Magistrate), 62
Morgan, Richard, 64
Morning Advertiser, 89, 153, 166, 168, 170, 171
Morning Chronicle, The, 149
Morning Post, The, 80

National Convention (see Chartists, National Convention)
National Political Union, 144, 147
Nelson, Mr John, 176
Neville, Henry (Juror), 69
New London Bridge Theatre, 165
Nicholson, Mr J., 169

Observer, The, 151, 171

O'Connell, Daniel, M.P., 151, 159, 169, 178; addresses Crown & Anchor meeting, 148–150

Parke, Mr Justice, 155, 156
Pearson, The Rev., George Fursey trial evidence, 159
Pearson. Thomas (Juror), 69, 169
Peel, Sir Robert, 29, 30, 35, 38, 39, 148, 172
Peoples' Charter, 20
Perkins, Mary Ann, 136; Inquest evidence, 101
Peterloo riots, 23, 28, 55, 63
Phillipps, Samuel March, 45, 48, 49, 173
Phillips, Mr, 155, 156, 158, 159
Pitt, William, 17, 28
Place, Francis, 37–39
Plummers Hotel, 51
Police Bill, 29, 30, 38
Police Committee, set up, 29
Police Conduct, Instructions, 36, 37
Police spying, Inquiry, 51, 142, 156
Poor Man's Guardian, 144
Popay, Mr (Police spy), 51, 141, 142, 156
Portland, Duke of, 102, 109, 111
Prendergast, Mr, 77
Public Health Act, 21
Public Record Office, 38
Purdy, William (Juror), 69

Redwood, P.C., 62, 63, 67, 74, 79, 115, 155, 159, 160; Injured in affray, 58; Inquest evidence, 77, 78; George Fursey trial evidence, 156, 157
Reform Bill, 1785, 17
Reform Bill, 1830, 19
Reform, Bill, 1832, 21, 69, 164; franchise before, 17; provisions, 19
Reform Bill, 1867, 21
Reform Bill, 1884, 21
Reformer, The, 52, 144
Reynolds, Mr, 70

Index

Reynolds, Thomas, 169
Riot, definition of, 41
Riot Act, 33, 41, 60, 71, 97, 101, 117, 129, 131, 137, 138, 141, 160, 161, 173
Ritchie, Mr, 166
Robespierre, Maximilien de, 22
Robinson, William, Inquest evidence, 104, 105
Roe, Sir Frederick (Magistrate), 62–66, 76, 154
Roebuck, Mr John Arthur, M.P., 151, 153, 178; addresses Crown & Anchor meeting, 145–147
Romilly, Samuel, 37
Roome, Mr, 65, 154
Rowan, Lt.-Col. Charles, 31, 33, 37–39, 75, 85, 91, 92, 100, 105, 122, 136, 139–141, 172–174, 178; appointed Police Commissioner, 30; background of, 31, 32; actions prior to Cold Bath affray, 43–49; at Cold Bath skirmish, 55, 56
Royal Sovereign, 166–168
Russell, Lord John, 19, 21, 22
Russell, Mr John, 137, 138
Russell, Thomas, 109

St Andrews burial ground, 61, 65
St Annes, Soho, 105
St Bartholomew's Hospital, 97
Sawyers Arms, The, 162
Scotland Yard, 31, 47, 51
Seditious Meetings Act, 41
Selby, H. C., 106
Simpson, Mr, 74, 82
Slavery, Abolition Bill, 178
Smith, John, 64
Smith, Thomas, 106
Snowden, Mr, 110
Spalding, John (Juror), 69
Stallwood, Mr Nathaniel, 44, 52, 61, 86–91, 109–113, 117, 118, 125, 137, 175, 176; called upon stop incitement, 60; evidence at Inquest, 70–73; asks leave correct part of evidence, 101, 102; 'Times' letter regarding fine, 106; Johnston awarded damages, 107, 108; tells Inquest of letter from Culley 'murderer', 121; 'Times' anonymous letter, 126; evidence at Fursey trial, 158, 159
Stamp Act, 25
Stirling, Mr Thomas (Coroner), 75–77, 81, 83–85, 89, 93, 95, 96, 98, 99, 101, 102, 105, 113, 119–124, 126, 127, 129–137, 147, 150; Culley Inquest opens, 68; Inquest verdict, 133; Jury asked reconsider verdict, 134; comment on verdict, 135
Stockton, Samuel Radmass (Foreman of Jury), 69; addresses witnesses, 80, 81, 83, 91, 93, 98–100, 113, 115, 122, 123; addresses Coroner, 85, 95, 96, 105, 113, 121, 123, 130–135; Inquest verdict, 133; receives medallions, 165; portrait, 167; Royal Sovereign outing, 168; presentation to, 169, distributes booklet, 171
Strand, 38
Sugar Act, 25
Sullivan, Jeremiah, 106
Sun, The, 66

Taylor, Mr, 154
Thames Police, 28
Thomas, Superintendent Joseph Saddler, 54, 60, 61, 71–73, 91, 101, 121; evidence at Inquest, 116–118
Tierney, Sergeant, 57
Tighe, Charles (Juror), 69
Tilley, Robert, 62, 63, 67, 157
Tilley, Thomas, 65, 67, 176
Times, The, 94, 102, 106, 109, 125, 137–140, 149, 153, 168
Tindal, Lord Chief Justice, 40
Todd, John, 140; Inquest evidence, 96, 97

Treatise on Police in the Metropolis, 28
True Sun, The, 90, 103, 104, 153, 168, 170, 175

Ultra-Radicals, 35, 39, 43, 77
Union Tavern, The, 44, 90, 101, 141, 175; Union leaders confer at, 52
Unlawful assembly, law relating to, 40

Venables, Mr, 73
Victoria, Queen, 45, 170

Wakefield, Mr D., 150
Walker, Mrs. Elizabeth, 109, 110
Webb, Mr G., 169
Wellington, Duke of, 30
Westminster Hall, 41
Whalley, Sir Samuel, M.P., 168, 170
Wheeler, Charles, 104, 140, 154, 162, 175, 176; Inquest evidence of injury in affray, 98, 99
White, Mr, 176
White Conduit House, 39, 163
Wight, Mr, 167
Wilberforce, William, 178
Wilkes, John, 25
William IV, King, 19, 38, 142; assassination plot,, 35
Winstanley, Mr Richard, 108
Working Classes, National Union of, 43, 45, 47, 64, 69, 84, 90, 102, 117, 140–142, 163, 173; Cold Bath Fields affray, 50–53, 56, 58
Worrell, Mr J., 108–110
Wren Street (formerly Wells Street), 44, 60, 70, 81, 82, 112

Yewett, James, Inquest evidence, 120, 121

For Product Safety Concerns and Information please contact our EU
representative GPSR@taylorandfrancis.com
Taylor & Francis Verlag GmbH, Kaufingerstraße 24, 80331 München, Germany

www.ingramcontent.com/pod-product-compliance
Lightning Source LLC
Chambersburg PA
CBHW070613300426
44113CB00010B/1512